The Ethan Allen Homestead on the Onion River in Burlington, 1787.
Painting by the author.

ADDITIONAL PRAISE FOR *AMBITION: THE REMARKABLE FAMILY OF ETHAN ALLEN*

"The Allens are one of early Vermont's leading families. We know a lot about Ethan and Ira, but not enough about the rest of the clan. Glenn Fay's *Ambition* does a lot to fill in the gaps. It's a useful and valuable contribution to the study of our state's formative decades."

-J. Kevin Graffagnino, Vermont historian, author, *Ira Allen: A Biography.*

"Vermont's extensive historiography concerning Ethan Allen has long required a single publication covering the many lives of those he interacted with from both inside and out of his immediate family. That need has now been admirably filled with Glenn Fay's *Ambition*, a one-of-its-kind comprehensive study of a diverse cast of characters living in an early Green Mountain wilderness. Highly recommended."

-Gary G. Shattuck, Esq., Historian

AMBITION

AMBITION

The Remarkable Family of Ethan Allen

GLENN FAY, JR.

Burlington, Vermont

Onion River Press
Burlington, VT 05401
info@onionriverpress.com
www.onionriverpress.com

ISBN: 978-1-957184-58-6
Library of Congress Control Number: 2024907514

This book is dedicated to the people who ensure the preservation of historical artifacts for public use.

Acknowledgments

Thank you, Michael Bellesiles, Phyllis Drury, Kevin Graffagnino, Elise Guyette, Gary Shattuck, and former governor James Douglas for your endorsements of this book. Your involvement pushed it to a new level of accuracy and readability.

A book that unravels a 250-year-old family story rooted in primary sources depends on people who are historians' historians. The UVM Silver Special Collections Library is the gold standard, and the librarians are the people who deliver documents and sources over and over again. When searching for obscure sources and hitting a dead end more than once, they deftly routed me deeper into the archives to find additional sources in their collections. Thank you, Christopher Burns, Prudence Doherty, and the rest of the team at Special Collections. Likewise, Mariessa Dobrick at the Vermont State Archives was very helpful in finding obscure records and helping me navigate their system.

At the Canfield Library in Arlington, Bill Budde, researcher and author of *Arlington, Vermont*, was enormously helpful in mining the Russell Collection during my study of the Sunderland years. Thank you, Bill, for the deeds, receipts, maps, copies, and stories that frame the Ethan and Ira Allen families in the Arlington/Sunderland area.

Sometimes, we take the availability of information and images in the archives of historical societies and museums at a reasonable cost for granted. Several historical societies and museums deserve gratitude for going out of their way to share their resources with authors at no charge or a nominal fee. In doing this, they reveal our history to the world. The Vermont Historical Society Museum and Library staff, especially Marjorie Strong, deserve my gratitude for assisting me with their sources and pointing me toward lesser-known materials off the beaten path.

Thank you, Andrea Mott, from the Poultney Historical Society, for the up-until-now obscure information about Heber and Sarah Owen Allens' lives and the historical landmarks in East Poultney. Thank you to Linda Hocking at the Litchfield Historical Society, who provided three primary source Allen documents at no charge. Gratitude goes to Colchester Town Clerk Julie Graeter, for access to the town's earliest records and maps. Thanks to James Miller, Archivist for the Sheffield Historical Society, and Donald Warfield at the Berkshire Athenaeum in Pittsfield, Massachusetts, for generous information on Zimri Allen. Thank you, James Haaf, for engaging with my research, deepening my knowledge, and adding stories to this project.

The Fleming Museum in Burlington provided access to Allen family memorabilia from their collections, including a miniature four-inch painting of Jerusha Enos Allen at no charge. Thank you to the Fleming Museum for all you do to advance art and history. The Ethan Allen Homestead Museum has provided inspiration and resources over the last several years as they have moved to a broader mission. Thank you to the dozens of volunteers, supportive patrons, and former museum director Dan O'Neil for keeping the museum and archives thriving and answering questions. Thank you to Executive Director Angie Grove for her advice and comments on an early chapter draft.

Thanks also to Rebecca Hougher, President of the Descendants of Green Mountain Boys, for her deep knowledge of genealogy and ongoing willingness to participate in unraveling the history of the Allen family and the Green Mountain Boys during the Revolution. Thank you, Suzanne, Skye, Nicole, and Pam, for your input and permissions for images.

Michael Bellesiles, who wrote his Ph.D. dissertation on Ethan Allen and a fascinating biography on Ethan titled *Revolutionary Outlaws*, among other works, was never too busy to offer his advice and support. Bob Bass, a researcher from Bennington, provided perspective and information on the 18th-century Grants and the early political landscape of New York and New England.

Legal scholar and author Gary Shattuck's recent and ongoing work that unravels New York Loyalist records and the 1770 ejectment trials is groundbreaking. Gary generously offered voluminous sources, informed conjecture, and reality checks rooted in his years of legal research, analysis, and experience. Legal scholar, Vermont historian, and author Paul Gillies offered exceptional insight and advice on the book's final chapter. The generous Vermont history scholar Kevin Graffagnino read a later draft, provided insight, and conversed. Thank you, Gary, Paul, and Kevin, for your intellectual power and informed opinions. Thank you, authors Jessie Haas and Willard Randall, for your expertise.

Writing about the colonists' relationship with the institution of slavery and enslaving Black people is complicated. Thank you to scholars Elise Guyette, Jared Hardesty, and Trey Williams for their valued reviews, insights, and advice on researching and writing about the Allens' relationship with slavery.

Sam Dorrance, a literary agent and an enthusiast of 18th-century Vermont history, offered generous coaching and advice. This book is better because of Sam's advice. I also owe a debt of gratitude to friends and fellow historians who took the time to read the early draft and offer sobering reality checks and advice. These daring guides include Terry Silva, Angela Moody, Tom Sharpley, John Achenbach, Danielle Davis, John Devino, Phyllis Drury, and David Cawley. Thank you, Print & Production Director Rachel Fisher, Sofia Silva Wright, and the team at Onion River Press, for all their help.

Finally, thank you, Donna, for editing and shaping drafts, supporting my interest in early Vermont history and my writing habit, and being a sounding board and literate confidante for my ideas and prose.

Contents

III

FAMILY TIES UNDER STRAIN

IV

ALLEN'S LEGACY AND QUESTIONS THAT
REMAIN

Introduction

In 1755, Joseph Allen, the father of 17-year-old Ethan Allen and his seven siblings, died suddenly on his farm in Cornwall, Connecticut. The oldest child, Ethan, was away at a boarding school preparing to go to Yale. He abruptly returned home to run the farm. Joseph's death undermined Ethan's college hopes and ignited his quest for answers to life's big questions and his lifelong political activism. His uncommon physical size, voice, eloquence, decisiveness, and charisma led him to become a militia leader during the 1770s in the Bennington area. His quest for a better life drove him and his brothers to be land speculators in the New Hampshire Grants. He became well known as the hero of Ticonderoga, an early founder of Vermont, and a best-selling author who chronicled his captivity as a POW. But the tales of Allen's leadership and accomplishments led to posthumous folklore that wasn't always accurate or deserved, and his whole story remains unfinished. Competing narratives of his life have rendered Ethan Allen a paradox.

This book tells the intimate story of Allen and his relationships and character gleaned from new research with a focus on objective sources. This version of his life departs from some of the folklore-oriented biographies that chronicle Allen's military heroism, leadership adventures, legendary intemperance, and feats of superhuman strength that were predominant in the 20th century. As a descendant of a Green Mountain Boy and a seventh-generation Vermonter, it is essential for this author to objectively study and portray Allen in his context and discover his true character and contributions. There are two central established Ethan Allen narratives.

Most of the earlier authors, including John Pell, Stewart Holbrook, Michael Bellesiles, and Willard Randall, began with the established image of Ethan Allen as a swashbuckling patriotic military hero who rose to national prominence as the courageous hero of Ticonderoga and leader of the Green Mountain Boys. Allen was subsequently captured and imprisoned in a twist of fate months after capturing Fort Ticonderoga at the beginning of the American Revolution. In these biographies, Allen helped found the state of Vermont. He later became a philosopher, penned high-profile books, survived his first wife, married an affluent and cultured young British Loyalist widow, fathered a second family, and retired to a quiet farming life. In the older biographies, Allen was sometimes mythologized and reported to have tossed bushel bags of salt with his teeth, bitten iron nails in half, killed an attacking catamount with his bare hands, and poisoned a rattlesnake with his high blood alcohol content, to name a few. Unfortunately, the colorful folklore has sometimes exceeded the objective information regarding his personal affairs, his life in Burlington, and those around him. [1,2,3,4]

More recently, several historians have pushed back on Allen's heroic founder image with a more sobering reassessment of his life that accentuates his narcissistic shortcomings, failures, and even legitimacy as a military hero and Vermont founder. Namely, John Duffy and Nicholas Muller delved deeper into Allen's life and writings and, in some cases, made conjectural leaps to reveal a starkly different Ethan Allen. Duffy and Muller claim he was an overrated leader with scant military training and experience. They believe the citizens quickly forgot him after he died in 1789, then "invented" him during the 1850s when Vermont craved a state hero. In their eyes, Allen's military blunders outweighed his shared victory (with co-commander Benedict Arnold) at Ticonderoga, and his British imprisonment revealed lapses in character. Duffy and Muller suggested Allen may have murdered an arch nemesis, enslaved Black people, and had intentions to sell out Vermont to Great Britain, primarily for his benefit. [5]

Another Allen biographer, legal scholar Gary Shattuck, wrote that New York claimed and surveyed Vermont lands in 1772, that Ethan Allen was a thuggish rogue and self-serving outlaw who failed to represent the Grants settlers with any legal argument in the 1770 Albany ejectment trials. According to scholar Harvey Amani Whitfield, Allen's spoken and written rhetoric fueled divisions that perpetuated institutionalized slavery and racism and made it more difficult for White people to see Black people as equals. Although these authors have sound arguments, they and others offer little objective insight into Allen's personal relationships and life in Burlington or those around him. [6,7]

Ambition departs from both camps, highlighting Allen's military and public life. Although it follows a narrative arc of Allen's life, it explores and integrates his web of personal relationships based on his surviving letters, legal documents, and other primary sources. This book summarizes Allen's personal life, close family ties, some of his political activism, and his lifestyle in Burlington during his final years. It also attempts to avoid the entertaining but often unsubstantiated folklore and instead relies on objective resources to tell a fresh, factual story of Allen. This project doesn't argue in Allen's defense but calls for less bias and more impartial empirical evidence. Some of the 18th-century images have likely not been published before. The relational context for this book is unique in other ways, as it poses several often unexplored questions.

What was life like for Allen's wives, sisters, sisters-in-law, daughters, and other 18th-century women in his sphere? What do we know about the dynamics between the idiosyncratic Allen brothers? What was life like for Ethan's wife, Mary, and their children in Connecticut, Massachusetts, and Sunderland, Vermont? What was the underlying basis for Ethan and Fanny's relationship, and what do we know about the family dynamics and interactions among Ethan's six surviving children? What did frontier living in Burlington entail in the Allen house as the Allens raised newborn children and farmed the intervale land (river valley) for two years before Ethan died? What became of Fanny and their children after Ethan's passing? Based on objective evidence, what was the status of his Black workers and the Allens' relationship with the institution of slavery, and what was his relationship with the Indigenous peoples? Finally, how did Allen and the Green Mountain Boys create Vermont's unique DNA that survives today?

Ambition also breaks new ground by exploring several key women. Allen's first wife, Mary Brownson Allen, has often been portrayed as an uneducated and unsupportive spouse. Yet, the objective evidence doesn't show that. Mary weathered many family storms and illnesses, cared for sick relatives, and raised their children on the frontier, often without Ethan. Brother Levi Allen's wife, Nancy, suffered from depression, living alone for years at a remote outpost in St. John, Quebec. Her correspondence reveals a coquettish relationship with Ethan. Surprising disparaging comments and compliments by Allen's siblings and children reveal Ethan's second wife, Fanny Montresor Allen, to be a complex individual. Not only was Fanny an affluent, intellectual daughter of a British Loyalist who had put a bounty on Ethan's head, but she was a mother and stepmother to six of his children. Letters and newspaper articles also reveal their parenting styles and divided family politics. All of these interpersonal dynamics occurred in the early post and beam houses on the frontier, without running water, secure food, or a stable economy. And what about the servants?

One chapter focuses on the status of three Black laborers who worked and lived with the Allens and the family's relationship with slavery. Weighing and sorting the factual evidence versus folklore and conjectural opinions about Allen's laborers is enlightening and complex. Although Allen's political writing disparaged slavery, was there evidence of anti-slavery activism? On a parallel social justice concern, is there primary source evidence to confirm Allen's reputed honorable relationship with the Indigenous peoples?

The final chapter examines a correlation between Vermont's genesis and its unique present-day ethos. Allen and the other Vermont founders' characters live on today in Vermont's distinctive (but not necessarily exceptional) culture and the ways we practice democracy. What unique characteristics exist in Vermont that began in 1770 Bennington?

This book portrays Ethan Allen and his family in a fresh light. It explores characters who inform us about the unique times of the unceded and contested territory of the Grants, which later became an independent republic and then a state called Vermont. It paints portraits of people who worked hard to carve a state out of a British manorial frontier. For all their faults, Allen, his brothers, and a handful of underappreciated colleagues were the key masterminds and courageous activists who stood up to New York aristocrats and forged their declaration of independence and governing constitution. At the same time, they lived active personal and political lives with great uncertainty. The factual evidence shows that some historians have overrated Ethan, and others have undervalued him. He and his family deserve more objective study.

I

The Allen Family

I

A Brief Overview of the Tight Knit Allen Family

On January 28, 1738, Ethan Allen was the firstborn child of Joseph and Mary Baker Allen in Litchfield, Connecticut. Within a couple of years, the Allens moved to nearby Cornwall to find better farming soil, and in that year, Ethan's brother Heman was born. The remaining Allen siblings would come into the world and work the land at the Cornwall farm until adulthood.

The Allen family continued the farm life on their owned land, and in 1742, their third child, Lydia Allen, was born. In 1743, Heber came into the world. Two years later, in 1745, Levi was born, then in 1747, the sixth sibling, Lucy, was born, followed by Zimri (also known as Zimmy) in 1748. Finally, in 1751, Ira, the youngest, was born. By that time, Ethan was 13.

Ethan Allen's birthplace in Litchfield, CT, 1738. From a postcard.
Public domain.

The Allens' farm life might have ensured survival in Connecticut, but it was arduous and not consistently profitable. Farmers had to be a jack-of-all-trades to be able to use a variety of tools to clear land; make, build, and fix things; care for and slaughter animals; preserve meat; and nurture and harvest acres of crops in an era before there were any mechanical tools, machinery, or soil management awareness. Livestock on New England farmsteads typically included a yoke of oxen, one to four or more cows, a bull, calves, mares, a flock of sheep, three to six hogs, a horse, heifers, and a yoke of steers and colts. Crops would have included medicinals, dyes, vegetable gardens, flax for linen, corn, wheat, oats, and other crops.[1]

As Ethan entered his formative years, his father, Joseph, openly questioned the church's doctrines, which engaged young Ethan's views on religion. Specifically, Joseph questioned the doctrine of original sin. He postulated that if the original sin was invalid, there was no need for the salvation offered by Jesus. By the time he was an adolescent, Ethan's doubts about religion had already solidified, and they persisted throughout his life. Joseph also influenced Ethan's values about his future vocation. Although the Allens owned over a hundred acres, Joseph had higher aspirations for Ethan, who would surely do better than farming if he were a merchant or attorney. And Joseph could see that good land became increasingly scarce as the Connecticut population grew. Joseph knew people could make money in land speculation, but he had higher aspirations for his eldest to go to Yale and further his education.[2]

Ethan had been studying liberal arts for a year in preparation for Yale while boarding at a school in Salisbury with a man named Reverend Jonathan Lee. The curriculum included Lee's New Light evangelical sermons, and Ethan learned a dynamic writing and speaking style. Ethan also picked up a fair amount of Old Testament scripture from Lee, which he later used to embellish his letters, political propaganda, and philosophical writing.[3]

Unfortunately, Joseph died suddenly in 1755, and Ethan's formal education ended. We can only speculate on the extent of the family trauma and Ethan's state of mind at that time. Biographers would later agree that the loss of Joseph fueled a search for spiritual answers that led to Ethan's quest to understand God and imbued his siblings with a drive for success.

At the time, the Allen children ranged in age from four to 17. Only Ethan, Heman, and Heber would have been helpful for farm labor. Levi would have only been about eight and might have been able to do some light work, but the younger ones still needed constant supervision, which 12-year-old sister Lydia likely provided.

Ethan returned home to run the farm and put his studies on hold. Ethan, Heman, Heber, and their mother, Mary Baker Allen, must have carried heavy burdens to continue the management and constant labor on the farm. Mary, who was 46 at the time, never remarried. The Allen siblings likely learned the value of working together and supporting each other, a bond that would continue throughout their lives. Ethan set high expectations for his siblings' contributions to the manual labor. Unsurprisingly, younger brother Levi later complained to others that Ethan had been a "dictator" while growing up on the farm.[4]

Joseph's estate included a 500-acre farm with only 13 acres of plowable stony soil, and the family endeavored to keep the farm together as long as they could. As the younger siblings grew, they became working age, and Ethan looked for new opportunities. As the patriarch of his family, Ethan would have hauled grain to the nearest mill at the Brownson family farm in nearby Woodbury, where he met his future business partners, the Brownson brothers, and his future wife, Mary Brownson.

Remember Baker, Jr. - First Cousin and Business Partner

Remember Baker Mill in East Arlington, VT.
The original mill burned in 1790 and was
rebuilt.
Author photo.

During the 1750s, Remember Baker was stationed at Fort William Henry at Lake George for a while. Ethan joined the Cornwall militia in 1757, perhaps inspired by Baker. Ethan's Cornwall militia unit was activated, trained, and marched toward Fort William Henry in New York to engage the French. But before they arrived, they met retreating troops with the bad news that the French had already seized the fort, and they returned to Cornwall. But only for a short time.

Baker continued with military service on expeditions throughout Vermont, New York, Lake Champlain, and Canada. In 1759, he enlisted in General Abercrombie's attempted invasion of French Canada. Under the command of General Putnam with Lord Howe, Baker's unit was out-manned five to one and surrounded by French troops. Baker's unit cut through enemy lines, killed 300 of the enemy, and captured over 100 prisoners. General Putnam named Baker for an honorable mention in the battle. Baker returned home and married Desire Hurlbut in Roxbury in 1760. By 1764, Baker had set up a mill in Arlington (presently East Arlington) in the New Hampshire Grants (presently Vermont).

Like Ethan, Remember Baker was thirteen years older than Ira, to whom he taught wilderness survival. Remember and Ira surveyed a lot of territory in the Grants wilderness during the early 1770s, working and mainly living off the land. Ira Allen's autobiography offers some adventures Allen and Baker experienced during these years. These stories give us a vicarious look into living in the Vermont wilderness.[5,6]

In one episode, Baker became separated, and Ira came face to face with a big white-tailed deer. Allen shot the deer and, not wanting to waste more powder to finish him off, grabbed the buck by its enormous rack of horns to cut its throat with his knife. Before he could execute the lethal stroke, the big animal swung his head and flipped Allen, knocking him down. In the excitement, Allen temporarily lost his knife. He regained the blade, but after a second attempt, Allen feared he would get gored. He grabbed his gun and "blew his brains out." Afterward, he skinned the deer and hung the meat up and out of reach of predators.[7]

Another time, Baker came face to face with a charging female bear, alone. He pulled out his ax and raised it to hit the bear in the head. The ax caught on an overhead branch, then glanced and hit the bear, causing a deep neck wound. The furious, wounded bear lunged again, and Baker managed to pull the ax out of her neck and hit her a couple more times to put her down without getting mauled. He skinned and butchered the bear, and they had plenty of food for a while. Baker bragged to Allen that he could eat nothing but bear meat for days. Allen replied that he could do anything Baker could. Unfortunately, that didn't always work out as planned.[8]

After a few days of eating only bear meat, stored at air temperature in a cloth or leather sack, they ran out and found themselves hungry again. Baker found some suckers in a stream, and he showed Ira how to catch the fish with a crooked stick instead of spearing them. Then Baker showed Allen how to cook the fish without gutting or skinning them, and they both feasted on their catch. A day later, Allen became ill with a fever and ague (chills), which was not uncommon. Baker subsequently developed a severe case of dysentery and joked that he would never go fishing with Allen again.[9]

On another expedition, Allen and Baker's party of four were on their way to survey the town of Mansfield, which included the rocky slopes and unfarmable tundra of Mount Mansfield! Although the mountainous terrain and poor soils were unsuitable for farming, Allen joked that his prospective out-of-state buyers didn't know this. Somewhere in the wilderness near the Onion River, one of the men named Wilkins carelessly planted a hatchet into his shin. They bandaged Wilkins up, made a "boat," paddled it upriver to the next falls, and then got out to hike around them. They walked and carried Wilkins to the next rapids, made a new boat (probably a canoe), paddled it as far as they could, and carried Wilkins again. Allen treated Wilkins using elm leaves, poultices, and other folk remedies. When they arrived at Mansfield a week later, Wilkins could walk without help.[10]

During another segment in Allen's autobiography, Allen suffered from boils on his ankles and knees. After a few days of worsening symptoms, Allen couldn't bend his knee, but he soldiered on doing the best he could. Days away from medical attention, he resorted to making and applying a leaf and bark poultice, and after a few days, his condition improved. He and the three other men with him were famished and hadn't eaten for days. One of the men, Issac Vanornum, shot at but missed a moose. Later, Vanornum did manage to shoot a partridge. He boiled the bird in a tin pan of water, added some pepper (all the food they had left), and split the "soup" four ways.[11]

The group had the good fortune to come upon a "camp" just as it began to rain. It continued to rain all night. One of the men, Elija Sherman, was convinced he heard a woman outside (it was a screech owl). He ventured outside and called out to her. Sure enough, she called back! Sherman called his companions outside, hopeful they might find the elusive woman in the night. There was no word on the outcome of Sherman's search.[12]

Remember Baker was a tough guy, a hot-tempered soldier, a Green Mountain Boy, and an Allen business partner. He built the first mill in Pownal, then another mill in Arlington, where Governor Chittenden, Ira, Ethan, and the Brownsons lived during the late 1770s and early 1780s. Baker was the first town clerk in that town, surveyed tens of thousands of acres, helped Ira build a blockhouse in Colchester, and was a partner in the Onion River Land Company (ORLC). Remember and his wife Desire produced two boys, Ozi and Remember Baker III.[13]

In 1775, at age 37, Baker was part of a scouting mission with Captain Seth Warner on the Richelieu River in Canada. He became isolated, and Indians killed and beheaded him. In 1778, his wife Desire and the two boys moved down the road to Ira's house in Sunderland, where they lived for a few years.[14]

Unfortunately, of all the Allen siblings, only Ethan, Levi, and Ira left behind autobiographies that survive today. The three memoirs differ in style and detail, but their family was central in their lives. Ira had written an extensive tome but lost the first portion of the manuscript about his childhood before it was published. Like many families, their stories offer a glimpse of their close family ties that eventually eroded. Understanding one sibling is only possible in the context of the others. Here is a summary of the Allen family of siblings.

The Family of Joseph Allen and Mary Baker Allen:

Joseph Allen (1708-1755) married (1737) Mary Baker (1709-1774)

Ethan Allen (1738-1789)

Heman Allen (1740-1778)

Lydia Allen Finch (1742-1770)

Heber Allen (1743-1782)

Levi Allen (1745-1801)

Lucy Allen Beebe (1747-1775)

Zimri Allen (1748-1776)

Ira Allen (1751-1814)[15]

2

Ethan Allen 1738-1789

The New Hampshire Grants, or "the Grants" (presently Vermont), were the land of opportunity as far as the Allens were concerned, and with good reason. Between 1760 and 1764, New Hampshire governor Benning Wentworth issued 112 new townships and 16 more by 1767 when he left office. At that time, one could buy an entire town for 20 to 40 English pounds. None of the Allens had that kind of money. Still, their father Joseph's enduring message of the importance of land ownership and profits from speculation echoed with the Allens as they matured into adulthood. Most Allen scholars believe this set the stage for the Allens to eventually acquire large swaths of the Grants, hoping to raise their families and improve their lifestyles and status.

On the frontier, boys of modest economic means often lived at home with their families, saving whatever money they could until they were 21 or older. When the time came, once they could afford a roof over their heads, many would seek a bride, hope to buy land, build a cabin out of native trees, clear the land, and farm it. Historians say that at least 60 acres were needed to sustain a farm. They hoped to clear a few acres out of the forest yearly. The seemingly endless trees would be used as lumber or burned to make potash, a desirable commodity in high demand. The undisturbed topsoil in the northern virgin forests was rich and fertile for growing crops until settlers eventually depleted the soil and the timber. Clearcutting forests is usually considered an environmental disaster today. Ethan Allen was also interested in intellectual pursuits.

In 1760, Allen was 22, and within a year or two, he met Dr. Thomas Young, a physician and avid deist slightly older than Allen. Today, Deism, a belief in a supreme creator that doesn't intervene with humanity, is not far out of the mainstream of American spiritual beliefs. But, during the 18th century, few philosophers were willing to challenge scripture, particularly the Calvinistic church, which had great political power in the colonies and communities. Even though Washington, Jefferson, Franklin, Madison, and Monroe were considered Deists, they didn't take a public stand and attempt to make it a political issue like Ethan did.

It turned out that Allen's friend and mentor, Dr. Young, was also a strong proponent of the Patriot cause, a member of the Boston Committee of Correspondence, and the Sons of Liberty. Young participated in the Boston Tea Party as a diversion from the main event by reading a prepared speech. Young and Allen engaged in many conversations about philosophy and religion over the years, and the two became good friends. Young may have filled a gap left by Allen's deceased father, and the two men had similar interests in their quest to understand the world and fight for the Patriot cause.

The two worked on putting their ideas on paper over the years, and some scholars presume they intended to culminate their work in a book. Dr. Young's biographers claim the two men agreed that the surviving one would publish their ideas. The collaboration is a plausible explanation for the genesis of Allen's future book, *Reason the Only Oracle of Man: Or, A Compenduous System of Natural Religion (Reason)*.[1,2,3]

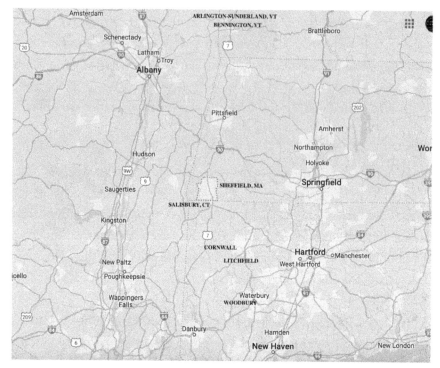

Map of Cornwall, Litchfield, Woodbury, and Salisbury, CT; Sheffield and Northampton, MA; and Bennington, Arlington, and Sunderland, VT. Note how most towns the Allens lived in sit adjacent to present-day Route 7, running north and south.

Google image.

In 1762, the enterprising brothers Ethan and Heman became partners with three other men in purchasing part of the iron-rich Tohconnick Mountain near Salisbury, which included timber and water rights. Ethan lived in a large house near the mining site, and the partners built an iron furnace to make potash kettles and other iron goods. It was the first iron furnace in Connecticut and employed 50 men. In a dozen years, it would be a significant producer of cannons during the Revolutionary War. That same year, Ethan and Mary Brownson married in June. The following year, their first child, Lorraine, was born.[4]

Although the iron business was booming, Ethan became locally unpopular due to his oppositional personality and outspoken views on the church. He publicly clashed with influential pastors in Salisbury and was articulate and persuasive enough to raise concern among the clergy that he might threaten their establishment. Although Connecticut had outlawed smallpox vaccinations, Allen had his friend Dr. Young publicly inoculate him in front of the Salisbury meetinghouse on a Sunday in 1764. Following church beliefs, this was forbidden by the town.

After being threatened with prosecution, Allen made some vociferous comments repudiating scripture, disparaging Jesus Christ, and announcing he wished he was bound down in hell with "Belzabub" and "insipid devils for a thousand years." After that episode, the town tried Ethan for blasphemy, and he became socially ostracized in Salisbury.[5,6]

In October 1765, Ethan and Heman sold their shares in the iron forge and house for a slim profit. Unfortunately, there was some miscommunication with the buyer regarding the terms of the sale. Ethan expected to get more cash up front, and a dispute ensued with the buyer, George Caldwell. The dispute escalated. According to court records, the 27-year-old Allen verbally threatened and assaulted Caldwell, then stripped himself naked and, in all the excitement, punched Caldwell. Caldwell took legal action, and the judge fined Allen for assaulting Caldwell.[7]

If that wasn't enough, a second encounter occurred with Caldwell and Allen on the road outside town a month afterward. Allen was still bitter about what he believed was a bad real estate deal. The two men argued, and tempers flared. Ethan again stripped off his clothes to his naked body, held up his fist in a threatening manner, and repeatedly shouted, "You lie like a dog!" He also shouted that he would spill the blood of anyone who opposed him. After this encounter, Justice Hutchinson, who had levied the original fine, agreed to dismiss the charges if Allen left Salisbury.[8]

While Heman and Levi used some of the modest profit from the forge and house sale to open a store in Salisbury, Ethan moved his family to Northampton, Massachusetts, where his grandparents had lived. He used part of his profits from the iron venture to buy shares in a lead mine in Northampton with his brothers-in-law, Abraham and Israel Brownson, and some other men.

Allen and the Brownsons worked as business partners along with politician, lawyer, and enslaver Benjamin Stiles. In their critical book,

Inventing Ethan Allen, John Duffy and Nick Muller assert, without evidence, that Allen supervised enslaved men Tom, Cato, and Cesar and that they "could have been hired out" for work in the mine. Although it is plausible that enslaved labor would be an asset in arduous lead mine work, Duffy and Muller's cited sources don't show this scenario.

Unfortunately, the lead ore didn't pan out, the new mining venture quickly lost money, and the Brownsons couldn't sustain the payroll. As a result, Allen was owed money and found himself in debt and at odds with the Brownson brothers. But this was only part of Allen's problems.

The town of Northampton was the main stage of The Great Awakening religious revival, which featured the legendary Reverend Jonathan Edwards of the Congregational Church. As usual, Allen was not shy in sharing his religious skepticism and criticism about religion in taverns and social circles. Although Ethan's little brother Ira and others were fined and imprisoned for "breeching the Sabbath," [sic], i.e., traveling on a Sunday, Ethan seemed inspired to battle the church. He was warned several times not to forcefully publicly announce his views. Many citizens began to object to his conduct, and in July of 1767, at a town meeting, Northampton officially ordered Allen and his family to leave town. He immediately moved his family to Salisbury to live over Heman's store.[9]

To add to the stress, the Brownsons could still not pay Ethan his overdue wages from the sinking lead mine. He sued them to recover wages. They counter-sued to regain some of the equipment he had removed from the mine. Allen did win back a small portion of his wages. Unfortunately, as we shall see in the next chapter, Allen decided to hold on to some other Brownson possessions as collateral. Trouble seemed to follow him, and things were heating up in the colonies.

Friction was building between British forces and the ordinary people, and the 1760s became a tumultuous decade. Just over the Connecticut border, in Dutchess County, New York, a manorial system of land ownership, begun by the Dutch and continued by the British, meant aspiring farmers had to lease their land and water rights from wealthy aristocratic landlords. The Allens knew the difference between leasing and buying land that would appreciate with sweat equity over time. They believed the New York manorial system was an unprofitable and fruitless deal for small farmers.

In 1766, William Prendergrast, one of those farmers, was tried for high treason after protesting the New York manorial system. In the nearby town of Poughkeepsie, Prendergrast was convicted and sentenced to death by hanging, genital mutilation, and quartering. Fortunately for Mr. Prendergrast, he was eventually pardoned by the King. But this event was a preview for the land dispute conflicts that soon erupted between New York and the New Hampshire Grants (what is now Vermont) to the north. The Allens and their fellow citizens were aware of the civil disobedience and clashes with authorities and mindful of the potentially dire consequences.[10]

In 1767, Ethan Allen headed north into the Grants to hunt and join Remember Baker in the Arlington wilderness, where Baker had built a mill. The nearby town Bennington was an established and booming community, and the wilderness towns to the north were beckoning settlers who wanted to buy cheap land and build a homestead. Poultney, Arlington, Sunderland, Manchester, Tinmouth, and Castleton were appealing, to name a few. At that point, Allen intended to make a living hunting deer in the wilderness. Legend says he became acquainted with the Indians there, learned some of their customs, and became familiar with their paths through the Grants' valleys, hills, and mountains.

Meanwhile, Heman and Levi had a ready market for beaver fur for hats, deerskins, and leather goods from the Grants to process in their tannery and sell in their Salisbury store. They were a successful enterprise and enjoyed cash flow and many promissory notes. They also employed the Allen sisters, as shown in the invoices and receipts in the Allen Family Papers.

Little brother Heber was still running the Allen family farm at 25, but change was coming. On March 17, 1768, he married Sarah Owen in her native town of Salisbury. She was the oldest of 7 children born to Elijah and Patience (Wright) Owen. They moved 40 miles away to

Woodbury and farmed there for a few years before moving to the Grants a few years later.

In early 1769, Ethan and Levi headed north into the Grants to hunt deer and other fur-bearing animals with the intention of trading pelts, leaving Ira, Zimri, and their three sisters with their mother, Mary Baker Allen, on the family's Cornwall farm. Levi and Ethan both recounted their father and Thomas Young expounding on the virtues of land speculation. Buying and selling land was an easier and more profitable lifestyle than the manual labor of farming. It was time to begin their quest to buy land.

During the decade of the 1760s, Ethan and Mary had begun creating a family. Their children included Lorraine (1763), delivered in Cornwall at the Allen farm; Joseph, born (1765) in Heman's home in Salisbury; and Lucy Caroline (1768) in Salisbury. MaryAnn (1775) and Pamela (1779) would be born later in Sheffield, Massachusetts and Sunderland, Vermont, respectively.

Only Lucy Caroline and Pamela survived to adulthood. Lucy Caroline would marry Samuel Hitchcock and have a large family, who we will mention shortly. Pamela would marry a man named Eleazer Keyes in 1803. They produced two children, Chester and Allen, during the following few years. Mary Brownson Allen certainly had her hands full, and it is clear that Ethan did not spend much time at home playing a supportive role during their marriage.

While hunting and land prospecting in the southern Grants, Ethan became popular with the local crowd at the Catamount Tavern, near his rented house in Bennington. He was well-versed in the political turmoil and protests across the Connecticut border in New York, where small farmers were revolting against the New York manorial system. Some of those farmers had moved east into the Grants.

New resistance started brewing when New York officials began demanding rents, quitrents, and taxes from New Hampshire Grants landowners. Bennington had been chartered in 1749 and was a well-established town by 1770, with a population of over 1,000 residents and thousands more in the outlying settlements. But a succession of New

York governors were sending sheriffs into the Grants and demanding settlers pay "confirmatory fees" to New York to confirm or validate the lots they had already purchased from New Hampshire Governor Benning Wentworth.

Governor Wentworth chartered Arlington, Sunderland, Manchester, and other townships in 1761. At the same time, powerful aristocratic New York governors and assemblymen such as James Duane and John Munro had been given large tracts of land in the Grants by the King's governors. The New York owners had a vested interest in their land in the Grants, believed they owned the land, and had established New York counties in the Grants territory eastward from Albany to the Connecticut River. This disagreement created a monumental conflict between New York and New Hampshire and the yeoman settlers trying to improve their pitches. The settlers were emigrating primarily from Connecticut and Massachusetts.

Conflicts arose when New York sheriffs rode into the Bennington area to impose fees or claim their land and when agents attempted to sell New York patents or leases to settlers who had already purchased New Hampshire grants. During meetings held in the Catamount Tavern, local men formed a Bennington militia to resist the "Yorkers" forcibly.

By 1770, the big, burly, bold, articulate, opinionated 32-year-old Ethan Allen had attracted a following and became the militia leader. He was the right man in the right place at the right time to stand up and lead the Bennington Militia against the Loyalist Yorkers. While Ethan was engaged in Bennington, his brothers sought other ways to use their retail skills.

What were the other siblings doing at this time? Lucy lost her baby and died in 1770 after moving to Sheffield, Massachusetts. In September, at 18, little brother Ira helped Heman and Levi buy 350 pigs, and Ira supervised fattening them for the market, then drove the hogs 80 miles to Hatfield, Massachusetts, to sell. In September of the following year, Ira drove 150 hogs to Albany, NY, after spending the winter in Massachusetts caring for the herd.[11]

On May 29, 1770, Ethan made his first foray into real estate in the Grants and bought one right (350 acres) in Poultney for four pounds and a right in Castleton for six pounds. Typically, speculators would buy New Hampshire land with the deeded stipulation that they build a "shanty" or cabin, improve it, donate a nominal amount of corn to the town, and reserve the tall pines for the King's ship masts. The Allens had an investment strategy and hoped it would only be a matter of time before they could subdivide the land, improve it, sell it, and make money. Although Poultney was 55 miles and several days or more by oxcart north of Bennington, the land was more affordable than Bennington, which had become settled and appreciated in value.

The 1770 New York ejectment trials in Albany marked another significant, high-profile life event for Ethan and the state of Vermont. New York title holders to land in the Grants had brought suit against nine settlers who had bought what they thought were legitimate grants from New Hampshire Governor Benning Wentworth or his nephew, Governor John Wentworth. The plaintiffs hired Allen and attorneys Jared Ingersoll and Peter Sylvester to represent them against the state of New York. Allen didn't have a solid legal argument to defend the plaintiffs, and the trial quickly ended with a win for New York.[12]

Nick Muller wrote that if the Vermonters had deemed the New York courts fair and the New Hampshire title holders arrived at an accommodation with New York, they would not have needed the Green Mountain Boys. In that case, Vermont might have remained the northeast corner of the Empire State. "The Ejectment Trials and Ethan Allen's heroic rejection of Yorker blandishments, the decision to resist New York authority, and his spirited leadership of a guerilla campaign in the logical sequence adopted by most historians forestalled that possibility and gave rise to Vermont."[13]

After the Vermont defendants lost the case, New York officials offered to hire Ethan to work for them. Ethan Allen never elucidated his side of the story. Many years later, in his autobiography, Ethan's brother Ira wrote that Ethan's reply was, "The gods of the valleys are not gods of the hills," and he invited the New York attorneys to join him in

Bennington where it would be "thoroughly explained." Although Ethan didn't describe the interaction, it's not surprising that this quote didn't match the New York account of the dialogue.[14]

Three years after the trials, New York attorney James "swivel eye" Duane described the trial and the subsequent conversations with Allen differently. He claimed Allen consented and agreed to some degree of compromise in principle. But later, Allen took a hard line against New York and vowed to resist their attempts to recover land or money from the Grants settlers. We will never know what transpired in the conversations between Duane and Allen, regardless of whether or not Allen took remuneration from New York or what Allen said to Duane when. The loss of the case only galvanized the Green Mountain Boys to fight any intrusions by the Yorkers, with Allen as their Colonel Commandant.[15]

Time after time, the Green Mountain Boys, led by Allen and his captains, disrupted New York's attempts to exert authority. The paramilitary group bragged that they used "night-rider tactics" but never killed anyone in their fight for honest settlers against entrenched tyranny.

In 1771, Ethan took his wife Mary, who was expecting their fourth child, and their children Loraine, Joseph, and Lucy Caroline to Sheffield to live with Zimri. The same year, he rented a house in Bennington for one and a half years. With all the conflict in the southern Grants with New York sheriffs and land confiscation, the Catamount Tavern in Bennington was the gathering place for the Green Mountain Boys. Mary never moved to Bennington, and there is speculation that she wanted to be closer to the support of the Allen family and the church. Ethan built a home for Heber in Poultney and talked his little brother, Ira, then 19, into selling his share of the family farm and buying land in Poultney.[16,17,18]

In 1772, Ethan, Ira, Heman, Zimri, and first cousin Remember Baker became partners in the Onion River Land Company, which stayed intact for 15 years. The company name is a testament to Ira Allen's belief that the northern Grants was their promised land. The Burlington—Colchester area, bordered by Lake Champlain to the west and the Onion River running through the middle, was their ultimate goal 15 years before the surviving partners would move there.

The move northward into the Grants was a turning point for the Allen boys and simultaneously a galvanizing time for the colonies. The Boston Massacre occurred on March 5, 1770, when British militiamen killed protesters on King Street in Boston. The Allen family's land speculation became their new focus while the conflict between the colonies and Great Britain continued to boil over into a full-scale rebellion against Great Britain. Within a few years, the War would dampen the real estate market as towns summoned militias with the threat of British-led raids on their villages.[19]

Allen's Brief Military Triumph

The 1852 statue by Benjamin Harris Kinney, is a fair likeness of Allen, according to Allen's acquaintances.
Library of Congress

Although the scope of this book does not include Ethan Allen's military career, it is hard to isolate it since it played a significant role in his and his family's identity, life, and, as it turns out, in the Revolution. On April 30, 1775, Heman Allen arrived at the Catamount Tavern in Bennington with commissions and orders from Connecticut Governor John Trumbull for Ethan Allen and the Green Mountain Boys to attack Fort Ticonderoga. As leader of the Boys, Ethan Allen immediately sent out word of a secret mission. As we know, 85 Green Mountain Boys, under the joint command of Colonel Benedict Arnold and Ethan Allen, captured Ticonderoga and the fort at Crown Point, 10 miles north.

Allen immediately became a national hero and inspired the morale of the American Patriots. We can only assume the capture of Ticonderoga was on the mind of King George III when he issued a proclamation on August 22, 1775, declaring America to be in a state of rebellion. In September, the Continental Congress appointed a secret committee to import gunpowder, musket locks, and arms. In March 1776, Henry Knox delivered 60 serviceable cannons to Boston to end the British occupation and blockade in Boston Harbor. The Ticonderoga mission triggered Ethan and the Green Mountain Boys' heroism and popularity. But Allen was only beginning to roll to historic prominence. At least, that's what he thought.

After an ill-fated attempt to capture St. John, Quebec, a few days after Ticonderoga and a bungled attack on Montreal in September, the British captured Allen and scores of his men. Ethan Allen spent the next few years on prison ships, incarcerated at the Pendennis Castle in Falmouth, England and under house arrest in New York City. By the time he was released, he had lost much weight and hair. Emotionally, he was a broken man. Upon hearing that his only son, Joseph, had died of smallpox, he wrote: "The death of my little boy closely affects the tender passions of my soul, and by turns give me the most sensible grief." In the event of his demise, he asked his brother Levi to see that his girls were educated.[20]

Most of the Allen family stuck together and supported each other throughout their lives, at least until Ethan passed away. The exception was Levi's Loyalist conversion, which created a riff, most notably with Ethan. Since they were often interdependent, knowing all of them helps us understand the strange chemistry between them. Younger bachelor brother Zimri had bought land in the Grants, moved to Sheffield, Massachusetts, and ran a farm there, where Mary, the kids, and others would live for a few years. Mary possibly cared for Zimri for a year before he died in 1776. Not long after, Ethan and Mary's son Joseph contracted smallpox, and Mary took him to Lucy Allen Beebe's husband, Dr. Lewis Beebe, to no avail. Joseph died of smallpox, and based on the law, he was buried following protocol in a sealed coffin at night, probably on Zimri's farm.[21,22]

While Ethan endured harsh punishment and languished in prison over two and a half years, Vermonters declared independence from New York and New Hampshire, wrote a constitution, the Green Mountain Boys fought valiant battles near Bennington and Hubbardton, attacked Montreal and Quebec, endured British-led raids, and became an independent republic. Life was different when the British finally released Allen in a prisoner exchange in 1778. Allen's wife Mary and their children had moved to Sunderland, along with his brother Ira, now the state treasurer under Governor Thomas Chittenden, who lived nearby in Arlington. Ethan wasted no time literally and figuratively getting back in the saddle, advocating for Vermont, writing about his confinement, finishing a book on philosophy, planning his future, and reconnecting with what was left of his family.

Heman continued to run the store in Salisbury until he died in 1778. Levi sold merchandise to the British Army and got into other mischief. Ira stayed active in tanning leather, milling, farming, raising and marketing hogs, and saving his money for a few years. He then became the state treasurer and the Vermont state surveyor general. Meanwhile, the Revolutionary War raged in the colonies while Ethan languished in captivity from September 1775 until May 1778.

This book will profile all of the siblings. Unfortunately, little is known about Lydia (1742-1770) and Lucy (1746-1775), the two Allen sisters, their individual lives and contributions to their families and communities. Surviving journals and letters are few and far between. Marriage records offer some information for those who were married. Family letters, military records, genealogical data, town histories, and newspaper accounts help us piece together profiles of some of Ethan's siblings. Because of this, nonfiction history about 18th-century women is rare.

However, we have a narrative of Mary Brownson Allen's life thanks to a short biography and other sources.

3

Mary Brownson 1732-1783

Mary Brownson grew up on a farm in Woodbury, Connecticut, as the eighth of eleven children who spanned 29 years from oldest to youngest child. Her parents, Cornelius and Abigail Jackson Brownson (sometimes spelled Bronson) ran a farm and grist mill 28 miles from the Allens' farm in Cornwall. The Brownsons were a religious family. Her father baptized her and three siblings, and all of them were active in church affairs. Farmers came to the Brownson Mill to process their grain into meal and flour and sometimes stayed overnight until the milling was completed. It is likely that Ethan and Mary first met at the Brownsons since he was the oldest and was likely in charge of taking grain to the mill.[1]

Mary's father, Cornelius, died in 1746 when she was 14, undoubtedly burdening the family. In the 18th century, a woman's role would have been different from that of her brothers, who would have managed the outdoor labor and grind of the mills and farms. Mary's role would have been to help her mother raise three younger children and manage the home. The housework would have included a lot of labor-intensive tasks that today would be considered heavy work, including making soap, collecting firewood, mending and making clothing, slaughtering and butchering small animals, churning butter, and all aspects of preparing food, as well as carrying water, cleaning and fixing things in and around the house that didn't necessarily involve brute strength.

Although some historians have written disparaging comments about Mary's personality and repeated them without evidence, we don't know the dynamics of their relationship. Ethan never wrote or spoke negatively of Mary. She also provided Ethan with the incentive of a dowry. Throughout those years, Mary would rely on herself to run the Allen home, at times caring for others, sharing space with in-laws and nephews, nieces, and others in Salisbury, Sheffield, Massachusetts, Bennington and Sunderland, Vermont, and probably other locations.

There has been speculation about whether Mary Brownson could read or write. Most early Allen biographers concluded she was illiterate since she signed an early deed with an 'X.' Others cited that daughter Mary Ann signed contracts as a witness and Lucy Caroline later wrote letters to her husband Samuel Hitchcock concluding that Mary must have been literate to teach her daughters to write. Mary Brownson Allen biographer Terry Buehner, who wrote a master's thesis titled "Green Mountain Women," concluded that Mary was illiterate.

Although public schools were for boys only during the 18th century, not all boys attended school, depending on their family circumstances. The only school options for girls were private schools or private tutoring, which would cost money and were only sometimes affordable for working-class families.

Living historians outside the Allen house in Burlington, Vermont
EAHM.

What attraction would Mary have had for Ethan? There was a common 18th-century belief that once married, men typically settled down and would be present as husbands and fathers to their children. Ethan's brothers Heman and Heber did precisely that. But Levi, Ira, and Ethan enjoyed independent lifestyles that seemed boundless. Mary might have been impressed with Ethan's formal education, his philosophical interests with Dr. Young, his charismatic behavior, and other traits. As for Mary's attractiveness as a mate, although she was six years older than Ethan, he gained a dowry and a strong-willed, capable woman to run his home and raise his children.[2]

Mary and Ethan were married in 1762 in Woodbury. Reverend Richard Brinsmade of the Judea Parish performed their wedding ceremony. A big feast and celebration with both families attending at the Brownson farm would have followed the vows. Afterward, the couple rented a house on the green in Salisbury, and Ethan began working for Mary's brother Israel Brownson (1735-1785), and they immediately started a family. At the beginning of the marriage, all was well. Ethan and Heman bought into an iron mine venture, and Ethan moved his family into an impressive big house on the property. But the mining investment didn't last, and Ethan became notorious in Salisbury.[3]

Living with Ethan took work for Mary as the years went on. Ethan's oppositional behavior was costing them money and respect in the community. In 1764, a farmer sued Ethan for impounding pigs that had wandered onto Allen's land, and he paid a fine of 10 shillings. The following year, a judge fined him for assaulting George Caldwell, who had bought the iron mine. Subsequently, as noted earlier, after assaulting Caldwell again, he was formally evicted from Salisbury. In 1767, Ethan was ejected from Northampton, Massachusetts, where he worked in the lead mine, for blasphemy. During most of that time, in a weak economy with little cash available in the colonies, the Allens had no discretionary income.

Ethan did not spend much time at home during the remainder of Ethan and Mary's marriage. The old Ethan Allen biographies paint Mary as challenging to get along with without valid evidence from primary sources. But we know that she supported Ethan when push came to shove. During the time Ethan was away, at least one domestic incident occurred, which tells us something about Mary's devotion to Ethan over her brothers.

Mary's brother Israel Brownson had stored a trunk of clothes at Ethan and Mary's house. When the Brownson lead mine folded, the brothers owed Ethan some back pay. Ethan decided to hold onto Israel's trunk as collateral until he received his past-due wages from the Brownsons. At one point, Israel and Abraham arrived at Ethan's door while Ethan was out of town, demanding Israel's trunk. Mary was caught between siding with her brother, who had stored his possessions in good faith, or siding with her husband, who seemed to be surrounded by conflict. Court records show that when a confrontation occurred in the doorway of the Allen house, Mary ultimately drove off her brothers with an ax![4]

By 1768, Mary's brothers Abraham and Israel headed north to live in Sunderland, Vermont, in the same neighborhood where Remember Baker had built a mill. Mary and the kids lived over Heman's store in Salisbury, Connecticut. In all fairness, Mary had a lot of weight on her shoulders. By 1770, she had three children at home: Lorraine (7), Joseph (5), and Lucy Caroline (2). Any excitement or novelty from Ethan's impetuous nature had probably worn off by the end of the 1760s.[5,6]

Mary Brownson Allen's sister-in-law, Lucy Allen Finch, died in 1770. The matriarch of the Allen siblings, Mary Baker Allen, suffered a paralyzing stroke at Lucy's funeral and moved in with Mary and the children afterward. Mary Brownson Allen cared for her for the next few years before she died in 1774. At about that time, Heman married Abigail Beebe, and Mary was the midwife for the birth of their son.

In 1771, Ethan rented a house in Bennington, but Mary wanted the support of a stable extended family. Ethan moved the family to Zimri's farm in Sheffield, Massachusetts, so she would have the support of the family and the church community, where she and the children worshiped. The early 1770s were busy years for Ethan and the Green Mountain Boys, and as far as we know, he rarely appeared at home. Mary and Ethan produced another child, Mary Ann, in 1772, and at 40, it would seem her childbearing years would soon be over.[7]

Some sources say that while Ethan was imprisoned from 1775 until the Spring of 1778, Mary remained in Salisbury, living over Heman's store, along with a growing clan of Allens. Zimri had no doubt lived in Ethan's shadow and often stayed with Heman's family. Mary was entitled to purchase family provisions at the store, and in effect, she acted as Ethan's agent, and Heman was obligated to honor her purchases. Zimri died in 1776, leaving Mary acreage on Otter Creek in Vermont. Given couverture laws and gender inequality, this was unusual at the time and presumably a debt of gratitude for her care of Zimri through his illness. When Heman died, his will forgave Ethan's debts, which probably included real estate and store debts aquired while the Allen family lived upstairs.[8]

In 1778, Mary's brother Elijah helped her move the children to Sunderland. Some historians say they lived with and kept house for Ira for the next few years, and once Heman died that year, his wife Abigail and their children moved in with Ira, too. In 1782, Heber's wife, Sarah Owen, and her five children also came to live with Ira in Sunderland.[9]

The Sunderland-Arlington area was exciting because, in 1764, settlers included Green Mountain Boys and several Loyalists. Two of the first settlers were Green Mountain Boys Remember Baker and fellow Connecticut native and Loyalist Jehiel Hawley. Reverend Hawley was not a militant Loyalist but was known for bringing opposing views and parties together. His inn hosted Loyalist meetings on one night and Green Mountain Boy meetings on another night. Hawley served as an Episcopalian minister in Arlington for a while. He was quoted as saying: "The question between the Americans and the mother country is not yet decided, each party has a right of thinking as he pleases; today these men are in our power; tomorrow we may be in theirs;... let it be known that we are Christians, whose duty it is to be merciful and to forgive our enemies." For the most part, with a few exceptions, the Loyalists and the Green Mountain Boys learned to coexist in Arlington.[10]

The precise whereabouts of the Allen family at any given time in the Sunderland-Arlington area are portrayed differently in different sources. Deeds show that Ethan owned considerable acreage bordering Ira's Sunderland property. The Hemenway's Gazetteer says Ethan had a house on the north side of the Battenkill River, and that house was reportedly torn down in 1845 in the same vicinity as Ira's home. It is possible that Mary and the Allen kids lived in their own house, or they could have spent some time under Ira's roof, especially once Mary became ill. Mary was a determined woman who believed in and sought the stability of the family. Throughout their marriage, Mary was assertive and tried to curb Ethan's sometimes reckless behavior. The fact that she defended her turf with an ax shows she had strong convictions.[11,12,13]

In Ethan's absence, Heman became the family's patriarch, and Zimri often fulfilled the role of father to Ethan's kids until he died in 1776. Mary cared for others, including Zimri and Mary Baker, and endured the loss of her children, Joseph and Loraine. Some historians say giving birth to Pamela at 47 in 1779 was too much for Mary, and she was never able to recover.

By 1782, Mary was in much pain and very ill. 1783 was a challenging year for the Allen family. Ailing daughter Loraine's religious beliefs were more in line with those of her father than her mother, who found support in the church. She died of tuberculosis a month before Mary. Sarah Owen (Heber's widow) and her children buried Loraine nearby in Ira's small cemetery. Mary died in June and was buried at the Episcopal Church Cemetery in Arlington. Ethan had been away then, but he returned for the funeral. Mary left behind three daughters, Lucy Caroline (15), Mary Ann (11), and Pamela (4). It is possible that they lived with Sarah Owen and her kids at Ira's home when Ethan was away.[14,15]

According to historians and Ethan's grandson, Ethan Allen Hitchcock, Ethan either wrote or hired a poet to write an epitaph on a marker at Mary's grave at the Episcopalian Church Cemetery in Arlington. It is possible that Levi Allen, who was an aspiring poet, is the man behind these lines. This poem certainly rings similar to his other works.

"Farewell my friends, this fleeting world adieu,
My residence is no longer with you.
My children I commend to Heaven's care,
And humbly raise my hopes above despair,
And conscious of a virtuous transient strife,
Anticipate the joys of the next life;
Yet such celestial and static bliss
Is but in part conferred on us in this.
Confiding in the power of Heaven most high,
His wisdom, goodness, and infinity,
Displayed securely, I resign my breath
To the cold unrelenting stroke of Death;
Trusting that God, who gave me life before,

Will still preserve me in a state much more
Exalted mentally– beyond decay,
In the blest regions, of eternal day."[16]

Of Ethan and Mary's children, only two survived to adulthood. Loraine died of tuberculosis in Sunderland at age 20. Joseph had died at his Uncle Heman's place in 1776 at 11. Mary Ann lived to be 16 and died in Burlington in 1790. Lucy Caroline would marry Samuel Hitchcock, and they had a large and relatively healthy family. Pamela married Eleazer Keyes from Pomfret, Vermont, in 1803. They produced two sons before Pamela died in 1809 at age 30.[17]

The Family of Ethan Allen and Mary Brownson Allen:

Ethan Allen (1738-1789) married (1762) Mary Brownson (1732-1783)
Loraine Allen (1763-1783)
Joseph Allen (1765-1777)
Lucy Caroline Allen (1768-1842) married Samuel Hitchcock
(1755-1813) in 1789
Mary Ann Allen (1772-1790)
Pamelia (Pamela) Allen (1779-1809) married Eleazer Keyes
(1776-1816) in 1803[18]

4

Heman Allen 1740-1778

Some would consider Heman Allen a dull man compared to his brothers, and unfortunately, he left a sparse paper trail to chronicle his life. But as we shall see, in the final measure, Heman was the family's most dependable and successful businessman. He was a quiet, respected leader. Heman ran a store in Salisbury, Connecticut, for many years. Unlike his brothers, Levi, Ethan, and Ira, he never settled down in Vermont, was arrested, incarcerated, wrote letters to the newspaper, publicly blasphemed, or challenged anyone to a duel. According to his brother Ira, his constitution was too weak to spend months in the forests, surveying, exploring, and living off the land. But Heman, with a name meaning "faithful," was the most stable and financially successful. Furthermore, he was the diplomatic statesman of the Allen boys.

Although Heman was less high-profile than Ethan, Levi, or Ira, he was dependable and capable. After growing up and working on the family farm, he served as an officer in the Green Mountain Boys and participated in the attack on Fort Ticonderoga. Heman married Abigail Beebe, fathered children, and served as a delegate to the early conventions between 1775 and 1777 as a property owner. He served as a captain in Warner's Regiment under Philip Schuyler in 1775 and 1776. He and Ira served on the 12-man Committee of Safety for Vermont. In

1777, the Vermont Assembly selected him to ride down to Philadelphia and present a petition for statehood to the Continental Congress.[1,2]

Arriving at the Continental Congress in Philadelphia, 1776
Author photo, from a painting by Peter Huntoon

Around 1773, Heman trekked to Vermont to visit Ira at Onion River, taking the overland route on the newly cleared path that Ira had recently made (today's Route 7). The two brothers set out by canoe to explore the "Burlington pine plain," as Ira called it. They paddled down the river to the lake, along the beautiful cliff coastline of what would be named Sunset Cliff, Appletree Point, Rock Point, North Beach, and Burlington Bay–without a soul in sight. Along their journey south, they stopped to spend the night in Shelburne Bay and found an empty log cabin at the "Potiers."[3]

Not long before this episode, Ira and a few other Green Mountain Boys had sent a New York survey team packing with a death threat warning. As a result, Ira had become more wary of the possibility of Yorkers returning to capture him and bring him to justice in Albany. Heman and Ira slept on loose straw on the cabin floor. Ira had a habit of sleeping on his holstered pistols, which he usually wore on his hips during the daytime. During the night, Heman awoke to Ira crouching on his knees and elbows, facing the open door, a pistol in each hand. Ira cocked one pistol! Alarmed, Heman asked Ira what he was doing and, hearing no response, realized Ira was asleep and dreaming![4]

Heman awakened his brother. Ira recounted his dream that Yorkers were surrounding them outside, waiting to ambush and capture him just outside the doorway. He formulated a plan in his dream to slowly work his way out of his blanket, unholster his pistols, one in each hand, and make a run for it, firing as he went out the door and hoping to clear the woods. Once he got to Onion River, he would round up a party and come back to rescue his brother, Heman. The two brothers had a good laugh, happy to be safe. Unfortunately, after his rude awakening, Heman never got back to sleep that night.[5]

Captain Heman fought in the northern campaign in Canada in 1775-1776 and in the Battle for Bennington in August 1777. During his years of service for American freedom and Vermont sovereignty, Heman owned a successful store in Salisbury, Connecticut, and was also a partner in the Onion River Land Company. Heman and his wife, Abigail Beebe Allen, raised two children, including Heman, Jr. (1774), Beebe (1775), who died as an infant, and Lucinda (1776).

Lucinda would later marry Moses Catlin, an early successful businessman in Burlington, who built a house at the corner of Main Street and University Place at the present location of Morrill Hall at UVM in 1806. The farmhouse stood as part of Catlin's 22-acre farm for three years. But Lucinda wanted a house in Burlington with the best view. The Catlins sold their house to Burlington surveyor, designer, and builder John Johnson. The home became known as the John Johnson House and was moved twice, once a few hundred yards east. The University of Vermont finally moved it across Main Street to where it now rests, opposite the Davis Center.[6]

Moses Catlin had built a big new farm at the top of the hillside in Burlington on the present site of UVM Medical Center, where they lived for years, and it became known as Catlin's Hill. The area between

Catlin's Hill and the Onion River in Burlington was known as Catlinsbugh during the 1830s. They had no offspring but adopted several children, none surviving to adulthood. Lucinda died in 1848 at the Vermont Asylum for the Insane in Brattleboro. Mary Fletcher bought the Catlin Farm and, with the help of UVM President Matthew Buckham built the hospital in the late 1800s.[7,8]

Heman's household housed many of his siblings and their families in Salisbury during the 1760s and 1770s. Heman died in 1778 after a long illness due to injuries and disease from the Battle of Bennington. He is buried in Connecticut. The Heman Allen buried in Greenmount Cemetery in Burlington near Ethan and other members of the Allen family is Heber's son, Heman "Chili" Allen (1779-1852).

After Heman's death, Abigail married Solomon Wadhams, and they lived in Goshen, Connecticut, and had one child, a daughter named Melinda, in 1798. Melinda eventually married Guy Catlin, the youngest brother of Moses Catlin. The Catlins owned the Burlington Flour Mill at Winooski Falls, and Guy owned the Lake Champlain Steamboat Company and Champlain Transportation Company during the 1800s.[9,10]

Heman's last will tells us much about him and his relationship with his brothers, wife, and children. Heman had already balanced his accounts with Zimri and voided all debts with his other brothers. The store debts from Ethan's wife, Mary, could have been significant during the years she lived with the kids over the store, considering their financial troubles and the general lack of currency available in the economy.

Heman left his house, farm, horse, cow, 200 British pounds, account books, velvet, and two rights of Onion River Land to his wife, Abigail. To his "beloved brother Ethan," he left 500 acres in Georgia, Vermont, to be sold to educate Ethan's children if he didn't return from captivity.

Levi, Heber, and Ira each received 1,000 acres in ORLC land, clothing, and keepsakes. John (Ozi?) Baker, Remember's son, received 350 acres. Heman made Ethan and Ira co-executors and guardians of his young daughter Lucinda and left her half of his remaining notes.

In those days, a widow could not sell inherited land, or the proceeds would go directly to the children.[11,12]

The Family of Heman Allen and Abigail Beebe Allen:

Heman Allen (1740-1778) married (1772) Abigail Beebe (1753-1844)
Heman Allen, Jr. (1774-1776)
Beebe Allen (1775-1776)
Lucinda Allen (1776-1852) married Moses Catlin 1770-1842)[13]

5

Lydia Allen 1742-1770 and
Lucy Allen 1747-1775

Lydia Allen was the third sibling of the Allen clan. After growing up on the Allen farm, she married John Finch in 1764. They lived in Goshen, Connecticut. The Finches produced one son named John Allen Finch, sometimes called John Finch, Jr.

In 1769, the Allens sold the Cornwall farm, and their mother, Mary Baker Allen, moved in with her daughter Lydia. John Sr. predeceased Lydia, possibly before Mary arrived, or it is possible that Mary moved in to support Lydia after John died.

Lydia became ill while living in Goshen. During her illness, which lasted for a year, Ira rode a couple of days straight, switching horses, to get medicine for Lydia. On his return, Ira fell asleep on his horse at night and awoke utterly lost at a fork in the road. He guessed at the right path and shortly returned to Goshen with the medicine for Lydia. She passed away three days later in 1770. At Lydia's funeral, the Allens' mother, Mary Baker Allen, suffered a severe stroke, which left her partially paralyzed for her remaining years. Mary Brownson Allen cared for her in her household for the rest of her life.[1,2]

The death of his mother left John Allen Finch, at five, to be raised by the family as well. It is possible that he was raised by Mary Brownson at Heman's store in Salisbury, Connecticut, or at the Sheffield, Massachusetts, farm with Zimri. Both Zimri and Ira had close relationships with him.[3]

Zimri left him most of his estate when he died in 1776; John would have been 11 years old. Ira put John Allen Finch through Dartmouth. Other reports say Finch dropped out of Dartmouth. Finch sent Ira a letter from New York City to tell him he had dropped out of Dartmouth. He told Ira that God "has implanted in me a spirit of Aspiring to something beyond the level of Mankind... Have been tossed both by Sea & Land since I left Onion River, insulted, Cheated, nay my life indangered-& reduced in a Strange place, whence I had to rely on my wit, & as you know I had but a small share..." Finch worked for Ira at some point, and married a woman named Elizabeth. Despite his opportunities, he was not successful and did not live long. In 1796, Ira's wife, Jerusha Enos Allen, said of Finch, Jr., he was "a person of no prinsapil and abandoned to every fashinabel vise."[4,5,6]

John Allen Finch left one redeeming footnote for Ira. In the early 1800s, Finch's widow, Elizabeth Finch, moved to Philadelphia with her mother. Ira had cash set aside and managed to support Elizabeth and her mother financially. Elizabeth cared for Ira during his final decade as his health declined.[7]

The Family of John Finch and Lydia Allen Finch:

Lydia Allen (1742-1770) married (1764) John Finch (unknown birth and death)

John Allen Finch (1765-1799?) married Elizabeth ? (unknown birth and death)

Lucy Allen was the sixth Allen sibling. In 1769, she married Dr. Lewis Beebe (1749-1816), a Yale graduate from Salisbury. The following year, they moved to Sheffield, Massachusetts, and lived there for a few years. Some historians say they moved back to Salisbury, Connecticut, where Dr. Beebe had relatives. Lucy died in 1775 in Salisbury and is buried in Center Cemetery. The Beebe's only child died as an infant. Captain Heman Allen's wife, Abigail Bebee, may be related to Dr. Lewis Bebee, but we don't know. [8,9,10]

Lydia Allen Finch and Lucy Allen Beebe may not have been much better off than their female friends and acquaintances. Girls couldn't attend public schools. Girls from modest families such as the Brownsons and Allens could not afford to attend private girls' schools if they were available. Having the opportunity for an education and a life of improved literacy might have led to more empowerment, better lifestyles, and written documents that would have told their stories.

Preparing food over a woodfire was one of many tasks of women during the 18th century
Author photo.

6

Heber Allen 1743-1782

Heber, the fourth sibling of the Allen family, was born in Cornwall and grew up on the family farm. After marrying Sarah Owen in 1768, they farmed in Woodbury, Connecticut until 1770. According to *The History of Poultney*, Heber moved his family into a house Ethan had built and ran the farm in Poultney from 1771

The Eagle Tavern, ca. 1785, a Green Mountain Boys hangout.

Poultney Historical Society

until his death. Heber and Sarah's children included Heber, Jr. (1769), born in Salisbury, CT; Sarah (1771), born in Poultney, Joseph (1772); Lucy (1773); and Heman (1779). Unlike his brothers, Ira and Ethan, Heber was interested in farming, not land speculation as a primary enterprise. He was content with the life of a family man, farmer, and public servant.[1,2]

Heber became the first Poultney town clerk, eventually serving as an assessor and Rutland County Judge. In 1775, Heber served as an officer in the Green Mountain Boys during the attack on Fort Ticonderoga, the Battle of Hubbardton, and later at Walloomsac at the Battle for Bennington. Heber was in good company in Poultney. Seth Warner, Ebenezer Allen, Remember Baker, John Ashley, and other prominent Green Mountain Boys also bought land and settled in Poultney.

Every town needed a meeting place, and a short walk down the road from Heber's house on Route 140 in what is presently known as East Poultney sat the town tavern, known as the Stand. It was a typical watering hole for Green Mountain Boys. The Stand was demolished and rebuilt as the Eagle Tavern in 1785 after the war had ended. The Eagle Tavern building still stands, looking much the same as it did during the 18th century.[3,4]

Major Heber Allen was stationed at Fort Ticonderoga under Colonel Moses Robinson when Burgoyne's troops advanced up Lake Champlain to Capture Fort Ticonderoga, Crown Point, and Mt. Independence in July 1777. At that time, all the men in town had gone north to fight against the British Army. American General Arthur St. Clair ordered the American troops to retreat south. When word reached Poultney and other Vermont towns that the British were coming and the Americans were in retreat, 13 Poultney women decided to flee southward with their children to avoid the expected attack.[5]

Most women in Poultney walked several days and 50 miles (many lugging children) through the wilderness to Pawlet, then Pownal, and finally to the safety of Bennington during July 1777. Some women and children continued south to their prior homes in western Massachusetts and Connecticut. Heber's wife, Sarah Owen Allen, and her children were not among those who fled. Sarah stayed put, and thanks to Warner's Regiment, the British troops in pursuit of the retreating Americans never made it as far as Poultney. The retreating American rear guard engaged the British in the Battle of Hubbardton, the only Revolutionary War battle on Vermont soil.[6,7]

During the evacuation from Fort Ticonderoga back to Vermont, Heber suffered heat stroke and exposure that contributed to other long-term health problems. After suffering from chronic pulmonary tuberculosis, he died at his home on April 10, 1782. Heber's inventory included his farm, clothing, and household goods, valued at 103 pounds.[8]

The Allen family ties showed again as Sarah moved her children 30 miles south to Ira's place in Sunderland. Sarah followed Ira a few years later when he moved northward to Colchester in 1785, although some sources say Sarah lived with her son Heman in Colchester. In 1787, Sarah died suddenly in Colchester.

Heber's grave marker in East Poultney Cemetery reads:

This grave contains the remains of
Major HEBER ALLEN
Who with his brothers assisted in
The struggle for the independence
Of this and the United States.
He was one of the earliest settlers
In the town and died as he lived,
The noblest work of God.[9]

Heber and Sarah's son Heber, Jr., born in Salisbury, Connecticut, taught school in Georgia, Vermont for a few years and then migrated west. Their daughter Sarah, born in Poultney in 1771, married Captain Reuben Evarts in 1787. Heber and Sarah's son Joseph, born in 1774, would go into business with his uncle Levi in St. John, Quebec, although the business ultimately failed.[10]

Ira Allen sent their youngest son, Heman Allen, born in 1779, to Dartmouth. Heman graduated and became a successful lawyer, sheriff, county court judge, state representative, and Brigadier General in the state militia. After being elected to the U.S. Congress in 1817, Heman was appointed minister to Chile by Presidents Monroe and Adams. This Heman (of Colchester) was referred to as "Chili" to differentiate him from an unrelated contemporary named Heman Allen (of Milton), who was another successful Vermont attorney and leader. Heman of Milton (1777-1844) was born to Enoch and Mercy (Belding) Allen. As we shall see, Heman "Chili" Allen became a valuable figure in the life of his Uncle Ira, his family, Vermont, and the world as minister to Chile.[11,12]

The Family of Heber Allen and Sarah Owen Allen:

Heber Allen (1743-1782) married (1768) Sarah Owen (1748-1787)

Heber, Jr. (1770-1849) married (1798) Anna Hall (1779-1870)

Sarah Allen (1771-1840) married (1787) Captain Rueben Evarts (1763-1839)

Joseph Allen (1772-1855) married (1792) Abigail Cobb (1769-1835).

Lucy Allen (1773- unknown) married Orange Smith (unknown).

Heman "Chili" Allen (1779-1854) married (1823) Elizabeth Laura Hart (1800-1830) [13,14]

7

Levi Allen 1745-1801

Levi Allen was at times philosophical, humorous, passionate, emotional, obstinate, and violent. He taught school in Dutchess County in New York State, traded furs as far west as Detroit, ran a store with his brother Heman, served in the Green Mountain Boys, speculated in Vermont land, became a Loyalist, served as a British Army quartermaster, was imprisoned for trading with the British, was convicted and jailed for counterfeiting, became a merchant in territory that ranged from the West Indies to the deep south to St. John, Quebec, to Great Britain. Levi's memo books show thousands of records and transactions from merchandise that ranged from hats to timber, lumber, food, raw materials, textiles, and real estate. Levi spent most of his adult life on the road.

Levi's wife, Anna Allen, was always known as Nancy and came from an unrelated Allen family. She was born in 1748 in New Milford, Connecticut. In his time, Levi had a way with words and fancied himself a poet, an entrepreneur, and a citizen of the world. His plentiful surviving correspondences with Nancy and others reveal his passionate and playful temperament. He sometimes referred to himself with pen names, such as "Bumper B," or "Alonzo." He referred to Nancy as "Miss Snivel." While Nancy ran the store in St. John, Quebec, Levi traveled extensively. He was a heavy drinker, as his bar tabs and anecdotes illustrate. Alluding to Levi's drinking, in 1798, Nancy confided her "Venus" was jealous of his "Bacchus'" performance.[1]

Levi's first enterprises as a merchant involved the lucrative fur trade. He made dangerous solo treks to Detroit, trading with and befriending Indians, who protected him from thieves on the trail. Early in his career, after recruiting for the Green Mountain Boys in 1775, he found lucrative opportunities with the British. He was jailed for selling merchandise to the British Army and also served time for counterfeiting. While living in Connecticut during his 20s, Levi ran a store with his brother Heman. He owned and rented out a horse called "the Fox" at Thomas Bird's in Salisbury, Connecticut, and was involved in horse breeding and racing.

Levi bought an enslaved Black man named Prince in Dutchess County, New York. In October 1778, Prince escaped, and Levi posted a 20-dollar reward in the *Hartford Courant* for his capture and return. Eventually, Prince was captured and worked in the store in St. John after the war ended. The store sold dry goods, handmade animal traps, and beaver hats, among other merchandise. In one letter, Levi talked about Prince's competence and the value he brought to his business.

During his journeys and several prison terms, Levi wrote poetry on the state of the world, religion, and various other topics. Occasionally, he wrote poetry for his wife Nancy in St. John, Quebec, where she raised their daughter, little Nancy. During the cold, dark winter months, Nancy and little Nancy stayed at Ira's mansion in Colchester (presently Winooski). Records show that Nancy wrote letters and was literate enough to write fluently and transcribe letters for businessmen while she lived in Colchester.[2]

Levi owned tens of thousands of acres of land throughout Vermont, the Carolinas, and Florida, and even though he was not one of the original ORLC partners, he bought and sold land on their behalf on occasion. During British occupation, Levi operated a store on the harbor in Saint Augustine, Florida, was a quartermaster in the British Army, and traded in the West Indies. When Ethan was in British confinement for two and a half years, Levi wrote, sent him money, and lobbied for his release. He wrote General George Washington and offered to act as a double agent to free Ethan. Levi proposed Washington advance him money to infiltrate the British lockup "incognito." His plan included "raising a mob, bribing the goaler [jailer], or by giting into some Servile employment with the goaler and over faithfulness make myself master of the key..." Washington declined his offer.[3]

Levi's actions supported his reputation as the most violent of the Allen brothers, as noted by Ethan's grandson, Ethan Allen Hitchcock. Acquaintances told English businessmen not to be fooled by his rough appearance, that he was one of the ambitious and influential land-speculating Allen brothers with enormous tracts of land. He did not always present as a gentleman, and on occasion, he assaulted people and threatened to kill them.

Levi had a history of antisocial altercations. In 1778, when Ethan began confiscating Loyalist land in Vermont, including Levi's acreage, he protested, and the two brothers had a falling out. Ethan and Levi publicly feuded in open letters in the *Hartford Courant* newspaper, and at one point, Levi challenged his brother to a duel. Ethan's response was it would be disgraceful to fight with a Tory (Loyalist). Levi challenged no fewer than two other men to duels, including British Captain Edward Jessup in London and Levi House, a future Vermont legislator in Burlington. But none of his would-be adversaries accepted his challenges for a shootout.[4]

By the end of 1788, long after the war had ended and Vermont had welcomed Loyalists, Levi had reconciled with Ethan and embarked on a grand plan to win a British Navy ship mast contract. Levi and Ira hoped to sign an exclusive trade agreement with Great Britain and cut out the Canadian intermediaries. Contrary winds delayed his departure ship for months. During Levi's voyage in early 1789, while sailing to England, his older brother Ethan passed away unbeknownst to him. Once Levi finally reached England in the early spring of 1789, he failed to secure a navy mast contract and build a canal on the Richelieu River. After three years of being an American merchant in London and eating bread, steak, and a pint of beer every night, Levi decided to return to Vermont with a shipload of merchandise.[5]

"Foudroyant and Pégase Entering Portsmouth Harbour, 1782"
Dominic Serres, public domain

As fate would have it, contrary winds blew his return ship off course, and he arrived in the state of Georgia a month later than his expected landfall. Ira was his only remaining sibling. Vermont had joined the union, which he bitterly decried. The economy was stagnant, and his real estate empire had collapsed.[6]

Levi and Nancy enrolled little Nancy in the Bethlehem School, a Moravian Seminary in Pennsylvania, in 1793. They dropped little Nancy off, then continued their journey to South Carolina and Georgia. Levi attempted to collect debts in Savannah and disposed of 28,000 acres he had bought there. Two years later, little Nancy passed away at the Bethlehem School. She was buried in "God's Acre" in the Moravian Cemetery.

Levi seemed to be constantly in debt and became adept at avoiding creditors. Unfortunately, with his infinite appetite for acquiring land on credit during a sluggish post-war economy, bad timing and judgment, heavy drinking, and possibly gambling, his grand plans never took root or bore fruit. He attempted to become the leader of two new settlements in Canada, Barford and Compton. These projects both failed. After Ira was arrested with a shipload of rifles and cannons bought in France and headed for Vermont, the British arrested Levi in Quebec on suspicion of high treason. He was incarcerated in what he called "The Castle of St. Limbo." He spent a few months writing poetry, was released, and returned to matters in the States.[7]

During his final years, creditors closed in. He attempted to establish a racetrack in Burlington and advertised for a spring-fed spa he built at the base of the cliff on the Burlington waterfront. By 1801, Levi was imprisoned in pauper's confinement in Burlington. His attorney, Samuel Hitchcock, the husband of Lucy Caroline, Ethan's daughter, frequently visited him and attended to his perpetual legal and financial problems. Levi suffered a stroke, declined, and died in that year. Hitchcock administered his insolvent estate. As was the custom, Levi was buried in the southeast corner of the pauper's area in the burying ground on Warren Street, at the north end of the village, now known as Elmwood Cemetery on Elmwood Avenue.

Levi left five shillings to Ira, who "already hath enough," and most of his estate, valued at $33,000, to Nancy. Unfortunately, his debts exceeded his assets. After his death, with the help of attorney Samuel Hitchcock and others, Nancy Allen was granted 1200 acres of Canadian land as a former Loyalist by the British government and 30 pounds that Levi had paid the surveyor general. Records show she still lived in Essex, Vermont, as late as 1815. After being unable to pay an attorney, she became the administrator of her estate. No death or burial records have been found.[8,9]

On False Religion and Hypocrisy (last four verses), by Levi Allen

> Of commandments we read of ten
> Given by God for good of men
> He that by mischance break with one
> May as well break the other nine

The last line, what ungrateful Sound
The reason never can be known — found
Truly the old docktrine of hell
To draw men down where I will dwell
When a poor sinner has began
Why not repent, return, return
Oh! New England, vile religion
Enough to make *one* a heathen
Oh! What Shame from men to misses
Not one *believes* what he professes
False to *Almighty God on high*
And falser Still to men below
Their education all a crime
No more for I have the Indians blame
The Savage ideas far more pure
Of *the Gods* and works of *Nature*[10]

The Family of Levi Allen and Nancy Allen Allen:

Levi Allen (1745-1801) married (1778) Nancy Allen (1748-1815)
Nancy Allen, Jr. (1780-1795)

8

Zimri Allen 1748-1776

His family remembered Zimri as a man of ability and goodness. He was 14 years old when Ethan and Mary were married, and he joined the Onion River Land Company partnership with Ethan, Ira, Heber, and Remember Baker in 1772. The following year, Zimri worked on the farm and bought thousands of acres in the Grants on the side.

Although Ira deemed Zimri too slightly built to survive in the wilderness for long periods of time, Zimri had a strong work ethic and perseverance. He ran a farm, probably in the Ashley Falls part of Sheffield, Massachusetts. Although he was not as flashy as his brothers, the following announcement in the April 27, 1773 *Connecticut Courant* illustrates Zimri's personality and beliefs:

"$100 Reward. Escaped out of the custody of me the subscriber of Salisbury, on the 19th of April inst. Remember Baker of Arlington in Charlotte County, and Province of New York, and Zimrie Allen of said Salibury, being each of them under arrest for blasphemy, at said Salisbury on or about the 28th day of March last. Baker is about 5 feet 9 inches high, pretty well set, something freckled in his face. Said Allen is near 6 feet high, slim built, goes something stooping, dark hair; each of said fellows being armed with sword and pistol, and are notorious for blasphemous expressions and ridiculing everything sacred. Whoever will apprehend said fellows and deliver them to the custody of the sub-scriber, so that they may be brought to justice shall have thirty pounds reward of lawful money, for both, and fifteen pounds for either of lawful money paid by Nathaniel Buell, Constable of Salisbury."

On June 8, Allen and Baker responded to Constable Buell in the *Courant*: "Though we uttered some words that might be considered satyrical against doctrines that some sectaries of Christians believe to be sacred, Yet we are rationally certain that many of the pulpit thump-ers, in their solemn addresses, much more blaspheme the perfections and moral character of the God of Nature than we do."

This exchange offers a snapshot of Zimri Allen, encouraged by his 34-year-old battle-hardened tough guy cousin, as he and Baker articu-lated their true feelings for religion. A thirty-pound reward would then purchase several 350-acre lots in the Grants. There is no record of either man being captured and brought to justice.

When the time came, Baker and Zimri stepped up and participated in the capture of Fort Ticonderoga on May 10, 1775. Although the ORLC would eventually buy and sell hundreds of thousands of acres in the Burlington-Colchester-Shelburne area along Lake Champlain, Zimri would stay physically rooted on the farm in Sheffield, Massa-chusetts.

Zimri never married, and his property holdings in Vermont included a half-right of 175 acres on Otter Creek in New Haven (Vergennes) and 14 rights of 350 acres each in Hubbardton, which he sold on January 29th, 1776, shortly before he died. He ran the farm and sheltered his siblings and their family in Sheffield, Massachusetts, including his niece Lorraine and his mother. Two of Ethan's daughters were reportedly born on the farm. After a year-long illness, during which time Mary Brownson Allen took care of him, Zimri died of tuberculosis in 1776. There is no record of Zimri's death, but there is speculation that he died in Salisbury, Connecticut.[1,2]

Zimri's will reveals his sense of humor and family ties; it began with the phrase, "In the Name of God, Amen!" It spelled his name Zimry and noted his estate "wherewith hath pleased the Almighty to Bless me." He left most of his holdings to his 11-year-old nephew, John Allen Finch, Jr., provided Finch changed his name to "Zimry Allen French." Recall that John Allen Finch, Jr. was the orphaned only child of Zimri's deceased sister, Lydia. Zimri presumably requested the name change in jest, exemplifying his personality and camaraderie with John. He left Mary (Ethan's wife) a half-lot on Otter Creek in New Haven, possibly because she supported him as a teenager and, towards the end of his life, during his illness.[3]

Zimri left his brother Heber a half-share of a grist mill in Poultney; he left Ira 60 acres, clothing, and a saddle. Heman received a token book, and Zimri left Ethan, who was languishing in a British prison, nothing. Levi received a pair of leather gloves. After paying creditors, Zimri bequeathed four land rights to John Allen Finch. Based on the will, we can only speculate that Zimri's relationships with Ethan and Levi weren't as amicable. [4,5]

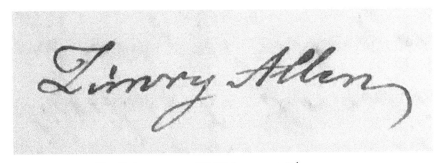

Zimri's signature on a ORLC Agreement, February 1774.

9

ⱺᴂ

Ira Allen 1751-1814

Ira, the youngest Allen sibling, was remembered as being gutsy, ambitious, a rugged outdoorsman, full of stamina, and always scheming. Ethan and other close associates referred to Ira as "Stub," probably because of his shorter height at 5'7". He was lean with black eyes and brown hair as a young man. He attended school in Litchfield until he was 17. Ira worked on the family farm and, early in his career, raised and drove hogs for hundreds of miles to markets. He became a tanner's apprentice, learning to process hides for garments at a fulling mill to be sold at the store in Salisbury. By age 20, Ira began buying land in the Grants, including two rights in Castleton and 32 rights in Hubbardton. He told the story of falling into a large impeller housing at the Salisbury fulling mill and almost being crushed. In another tale, he witnessed the glowing ghost of a headless woman at night that others had also seen.[1,2]

If the stories in Ira's autobiography are true, Ira became a robust woodsman who subsisted on salt pork for months in the Grants wilderness, exposed to the elements, working in the daylight, and camping at night year-round. Ira was the most dynamic partner in the Onion River Land Company (ORLC) and enjoyed a higher standard of living than his brothers.[3,4,5]

In 1773, Ira, Remember Baker and others built a 20-foot by 32-foot fort or blockhouse they named Fort Frederick on the north side of the Onion (Winooski) River on the present site of the Winooski round-about. The "fort," as he called it, was constructed of eight-inch diameter logs, a second story that jutted four inches out over the first floor, with 32 port holes, a roof that could be thrown off in case attackers set it on fire, and a "boiling" water spring inside. The fort had a double-thickness door, and while living there, Ira claimed he never ventured outside without a loaded "case of pistols" (a pair) in his holsters. Allen, Baker, and their associates lived in the blockhouse and hosted meetings there. It was an indispensable building for some time. How long did it last? According to historian David Blow, a December 10, 1783 deed from Ira to Baker's son, Ozi, mentions property south of where Allen and Baker's old fort stood. Based on that account, we know it had been dismantled when the war ended in 1783.[6]

Within a couple of years of the blockhouse construction, other men built several houses nearby on the north side of the river. In 1775, a British-led raid burned the buildings in the settlement, sparing the blockhouse. By the 1780s, they had rebuilt the settlement, and in 1786, Ira operated lumber mills and grist mills on the north and south banks.

Ira served in the attack on Ticonderoga and as an officer during the Canadian campaign in 1775-1776, including the ill-fated attack on Quebec City. He served in the assembly, wrote or possibly co-wrote the Vermont Constitution, served on the governor's council, and was the state treasurer for years. By 1779, Ira served as state surveyor general. Unable to pay him with money, the state of Vermont deeded the towns of Irasburg and Alburgh to him as payment for his work.[7,8]

Ira wrote dozens of propaganda pieces for different audiences, trying to establish Vermont's independence from New York and New Hampshire. He spent years traveling the state, successfully helping to get buy-in for a united Vermont from settlers on both sides of the mountains, and made several long trips to Philadelphia advocating for statehood. During the 1780s, he negotiated with the British for military protection after Congress didn't grant Vermont statehood.

In 1786, and probably before, Ira ran an operational sawmill to produce lumber and a grist mill to grind grains on the Onion River. A January 23rd agreement shows he bartered with John Daverson to operate the grist mill in return for a yoke of oxen and building a comfortable log house on the river. Ira was an early owner and developer of the riverfrontage and owned much of Burlington Bay. But as impressive as Allen's 200,000-acre real estate portfolio was, he was cash-poor and began to struggle to pay creditors.

In 1789, Ira petitioned the Vermont legislature to charter a college located within two miles of Burlington Bay in Burlington. He offered a donation of 4,000 pounds. The donation to the trustees included 1,000 pounds or 50 acres worth of land for buildings and a green. In addition, Ira promised 6,000 pounds in subscriptions from the neighboring communities. In 1791, the legislature chartered the University of Vermont, although it would be a few years before the first class of four students enrolled.[9]

Painted portrait of Jerusha Enos Allen, by an unknown artist, Artifact from the Fleming Museum
Author photo.

In 1790, Ira married Jerusha (Hayden) Enos (1764-1838), who was also born in Connecticut. He was 38, and she was 26, the daughter of General Roger Enos, the commander of Vermont's Mount Independence fortifications during the Revolution. Jerusha did her best to run Ira's business affairs during his absences.

Towards the end of the century, a depressing chapter unfolded in Ira's life. In 1795, he traveled to Europe carrying gold in the false bottom of a trunk. He aimed to secure a trade agreement with Great Britain and buy thousands of muskets and cannons to arm the Vermont state militia in a plan to conquer Quebec. The trade agreement was unsuccessful. After procuring over

10,000 muskets and six cannons from France, an acquaintance tipped off the authorities as he attempted to return to Vermont on the ship named Olive Branch. Great Britain arrested him on suspicion of arming Ireland or Vermont for military action against Great Britain, and he was tied up in court for a year.[10]

Once he was finally released, he was arrested again and detained in France for two more years after being suspected of being a spy. Meanwhile, the guns rusted and became useless. Ira's debts overwhelmed his revenues and liquid assets during his incarceration. He worked on his autobiography and wrote many letters to influential people attempting to obtain his release. In their letters between Europe and Colchester, Ira and Jerusha addressed each other as "my friend" and showed formal mutual respect for each other.

Unfortunately, when Ira returned to Vermont without his guns, his already overextended land speculation business was illiquid in a lousy economy, cash-poor, facing enormous debts, and involved in court challenges over the authenticity of deeds. He found himself selling off land assets and trying to appease many creditors. During the spring of 1803, he spent a brief period in debtor's prison in Vermont and faced certain long-term imprisonment for debt if he stayed in Vermont. All in all, creditors won settlements from Ira for over $2,000,000 in today's money. The Catlins, who were married to his nieces, ended up with his mills on the Onion River and built an empire in the Burlington area, a dream Ira never fulfilled.[11,12]

On a quiet Sunday evening in Burlington, Allen gave his watchful creditors the slip, and he stole away to a waiting boat on Lake Champlain. He sailed to Lake George, bought a horse, and rode south to avoid incarceration. A year later, armed with a bankruptcy decree, Allen returned to Vermont, thinking he was legally protected. Creditors immediately surrounded him, seeking cooperative judges. Allen soon realized he faced a high probability of incarceration. He escaped and settled in Philadelphia, where John Allen Finch's widow, Elizabeth, housed him.[13]

Ira spent the rest of his life there, separated from Jerusha and their children, with debilitating health. He attempted to recover debts, fight over 140 lawsuits, rally family members on his behalf, and instigate a revolution in Mexico. After hearing about the deaths of Zimri Enos Allen and Maria Allen, two of his three children, and suffering for years with retrocedent gout that attacked his internal organs, he died in 1814.

They buried him in a pauper's plot in Quaker Free Cemetery. Since paupers were buried without formalities or markers, his remains would have been difficult to find had there ever been an interest at that time. Unfortunately, construction subsequently disrupted the paupers' area in the Quaker cemetery, and his remains, along with the remains of others, were moved and have been lost. The Burlington newspaper only carried a simple statement of his death.

Ira had donated 50 acres and promised an additional 4,000 pounds to the University of Vermont. He hoped to make an additional monetary contribution and name the school Allen University. Although creditors drained virtually all of his assets, some historians believe Ira's nephew, attorney Heman "Chili" Allen, eventually managed to secure and donate the money Ira had promised to UVM. However, Ira Allen scholar Kevin Graffagnino doubts this. Heman protected Jerusha's wedding gift, the town of Irasburg, from creditors.

Jerusha and Ira had produced three children together: Ira Hayden Allen, Jr in 1790, Zimri Enos Allen in 1792, and Maria Juliette Allen in 1794. Ira Hayden Allen attended Middlebury College and married Sarah Parsons of Highgate in 1840. After Sarah passed away a couple of years later, he married Sarah's sister, Frances, who lived in Irasburg. They raised a couple of children, and Ira Hayden Allen was esteemed as a leading benefactor in Irasburg. He died at the age of 76. Ira's other son, Zimri, who also attended Middlebury College, died in Colchester at the age of 21. Maria passed away at 17 in St. Albans, where she studied at a girl's school.[14,15]

By the end of his life, Ira's legacy was full of contradictions. In addition to being a war hero, founding the university and the state, some of his business dealings were controversial. Money woes disrupted his family life as well. Although he housed, fed, educated, and cared for his siblings' families, he failed to execute Ethan's estate properly. He defended lawsuits brought by family heirs of his Onion River Land Company (ORLC) partners, including the children of Ethan, sister-in-law Fanny, Heman, and Remember Baker. Creditors ate up Ira's vast real estate holdings. Jerusha and the children managed to hold on to the town of Irasburg, which he had given her as a wedding gift, where she lived in prosperity. Jerusha died there in 1838.

The Family of Ira Allen and Jerusha Enos Allen:

Ira Allen (1751-1814) married (1790) Jerusha Enos (1764-1839)

Ira Hayden Allen (1790-1866) married Sarah Catherine Tilton Parsons (1820-1844)

Zimri Enos Allen (1792-1813)

Maria Juliette Allen (1794-1811)[16]

II

Homes on the
Vermont Frontier
During War
and Peace

10

The Sunderland - Arlington
Years 1778-1787

Ethan had first ventured into Sunderland in 1768, following the path of his cousin Remember Baker, who had built a mill in nearby Arlington four years before, and his in-laws, the Brownsons. He likely built a cabin or frame house with lumber that would have been readily available from Baker by then. The formula of buying lots, setting up the pitch by clearing forest, and putting up a house was the quickest way to "improve" land, or as we say today, build sweat equity. It was a typical pattern in land speculation. Ethan had earlier built a house in Poultney, given it to Heber, and likely built cabins where he bought land in other towns, too.

In the late 1770s, Ira Allen, Governor Thomas Chittenden, Matthew Lyon, the Brownson brothers, and other Green Mountain Boys moved into Arlington, creating homesteads, taverns, and stores a few miles west of Remember Baker's mill in today's East Arlington. Several settlers with Loyalist sentiments had relocated there. Hence, the Allens, Brownsons, and Boys moved into that town to keep what they called the "enemical" faction of Loyalists in line. The Hawley-

Crofut Tavern, still standing in Arlington, was the site of both Green Mountain Boys and Tory meetings on different nights.[1]

Ira was state treasurer, and his homestead was just over the Sunderland line from the village of Arlington. It was a convenient location and relatively close to the periodic conventions that alternated between towns like Bennington, Dorset, Windsor, Manchester, and others at the time. Remember that Vermont was still an independent republic and wouldn't become a state until 1791. Those conventions yielded the beginnings of Vermont's identity.

After 1777, Vermont repeatedly lobbied the Continental Congress in Philadelphia for statehood, to no avail. Ira, Heman, and Ethan, once he was released, among others, periodically made the 10-day horseback ride down to Philadelphia to apply formally, have the proposal tabled or rejected, and then make the return trip back to Vermont.

Mary's Frontier Life

While Ethan languished in prison from late 1775 until 1778, Mary turned to the church for support and baptized the children. Eleven-year-old Joseph died of smallpox in Sheffield while Ethan was still in prison. In 1777, Mary, with her three daughters, Lorraine, Lucy Caroline, and Mary Ann, accompanied her brother, Eli Brownson, to Sunderland, where they lived near the Battenkill River.[2]

Lorraine and Lucy Caroline were getting old enough to work, and there was plenty to do. Wood stoves and furnaces weren't available or used in the Grants then. Ten or more cords of wood needed to be burned in the fireplaces to stay warm through long winters. A cord of stacked wood is four feet wide, eight feet long, and four feet tall. Hardwoods such as maple and oak would burn longer and hotter than softwoods such as pine, but they were also more challenging to cut and split. The arduous wood cutting and splitting was time-consuming and was done by people who could work outdoors with hand saws and axes for hours.

There wasn't always plentiful food. The deer and beaver population had declined. Settlers possibly had bears, livestock, small game, and fish for protein and relied on Mary's or Ethan's brothers for meat. Mary's brother had a store nearby, and they made regular purchases there, but we don't know where the money came from. Mary may have had other workers besides the family in the household. Regardless of whether she did or not, Mary would have been busy. Producing, preparing, and preserving food was a full-time job. And there was little variety of menu options on the Vermont frontier. When they grew and harvested food, it would soon spoil unless people ate it immediately.

Mary would have provided their diets with fresh meat when available, which could be kept cold by hanging it in their unheated attics or putting it on ice for the short term. Most settlers' diets were protein-based, and they smoked or salted meat in the fall to consume it during the winter. They rubbed meat with salt during salting, placed it in wooden barrels, and topped off with water, making a brine. The brine kept the meat moist and more palatable than drying and prohibited the growth of harmful microorganisms.

When there was wheat flour and cornmeal, at least one day a week was dedicated to making bread, and that would only last a week, with big appetites and few storage options. Drying was the easiest method for fruit, vegetables, and herbs. Apples, peaches, pumpkins, squash, beans, corn, wheat, and berries were readily available and often preserved by drying. Vegetables and fruit were dried by laying them on a clean surface in a sunny area and covering them with a fine woven cloth to keep insects away. The sun or a cool "slack" oven could draw out moisture from these items, making them less susceptible to mold and helping them last well into the winter. After finishing baking, the cook laid the fruit on pans in the oven as it was cooling down, leaving the fruit overnight to dry.

Pickling was used to preserve produce. Vegetables and eggs would be put in glazed crocks, soaked with vinegar, and covered with either leather, clarified butter, or a pig bladder, which would stretch and act like plastic wrap. The family likely pickled every vegetable imaginable —even pickled marigold flowers for decoration on porridge.

Sugaring was another technique Mary would have used for preserving fruits. A variety of fruit packed in a heavy syrup would keep for months. They would scrape off mold growing on the top and scoop out the fruit. Sugar was inexpensive and readily available in 18th-century Vermont.

Mary would have made butter as a way to preserve milk. The cream that rose to the top of the fresh milk was churned to separate the buttermilk. Mary would have kneaded the resulting solid mixture and washed it until it removed the buttermilk. Even the poorest families with only one cow would churn butter to keep milk from souring. The household would have included churns, milk pans, and butter paddles. Mary would have relied on others for some things in Ethan's absence.

Mary and the kids didn't see Ethan from September of 1775 to May of 1778. When he was released from British confinement, word of his release took weeks to reach Sunderland. The day before Ethan arrived in Salisbury, Connecticut, his brother Heman died. Some accounts say that after spending a few days in Salisbury, word of mouth rumor reached Bennington, then Sunderland, that it was Ethan who died, not Heman. Ethan raced to Sunderland to head off the rumor, but it was too late. Primary sources haven't confirmed this story.

Ethan's Freedom and Reengagement

The British released Ethan in a prisoner exchange in May 1778. He was taken to General Washington's headquarters at Valley Forge and stayed there for a few days. He was introduced to some American generals and met polished continental troops who offered salutes there. After their meeting and exchange of ideas, Washington wrote to Henry Laurens, the president of the Continental Congress, on May 12th. In part, Washington said,

"I have been happy in the (prisoner) exchange and a visit from Lieut. Col. Allen. His fortitude and firmness seem to have placed him out of the reach of misfortune. There is an original something in him that commands admiration, and his long captivity and sufferings have only to increase, if possible, his enthusiastic zeal. He appears very desirous of rendering his services to the States and of being employed, and at the same time does not discover any ambition for high rank. Congress will herewith receive a Letter from him, and I doubt not they will make such provision for him, as they may think proper and suitable."[3]

Afterward, Allen returned to Salisbury, Connecticut, then later to Vermont, where he was met with a hero's welcome in Bennington. But the Green Mountain Boy presence that Allen knew before his prison term had eroded. Prominent officers like Remember Baker, Heman, and Heber Allen had died. Ethan's son, Joseph, who would have been a teenager, was gone. The hero's welcome felt different than it did in the past. At least Allen was free, but he was a diminished man.

Upon receiving word of his general's commission a few weeks later, Allen wrote Washington:

> "Bennington [County, Vt.] 28th May. 1778
> Sir
> I recd Your Excellency's Express this day, with a Bravet Commission; I Esteam the Approbation of Congress, your Excellency and my Country in General, Above gold and Silver. am now recruiting my Constitution, and for that purpose have Laid out a Certain regimane of Diet and Exercise. The Enemy keep their Ships of war Cruising in the lake but do not as yet Infest our Extensive frontiers, Tho it has been Expected that they will— they made an Attempt in March but were Beaten by the green Mountain Boys Three to one. I am Sir with the greatest Esteem your Excellency's Most Devoted Obedient and Humble Servant Ethan Allen"[4]

A couple of days later, Allen rode 17 miles north to Sunderland to rejoin his wife, Mary, and their three daughters, two of whom by then were teenagers. Allen's Sunderland home was just north of the meandering Battenkill River. It adjoined Ira's property, now a bed and breakfast accommodation on the west side of Route 7A. In 1778, Ethan sold some of his

Ira Allen House, Sunderland. Historians believe the left wing of this house on Route 7a was Ira Allen's Sunderland home. It is now a Bed and Breakfast.
Author photo.

Sunderland acreage to Ira. He also owned another lot and possibly a house a few miles south in Arlington, next to Thomas Chittenden's home near the corner of today's East Arlington Road and Governor Chittenden Road. A stone monument was used to mark the location of Ethan's hand-dug well. The marker disappeared during the 20th century from where it sat on the present site of a building supply company.[5,6]

About nine months after Ethan had returned to Sunderland in May 1778, Mary delivered their youngest daughter, Pamela. He didn't hang around Sunderland very much during the next few years. New York Governor George Clinton was itching to attack Vermont and settle the land patent dispute. General Washington had sent letters to American general Philip Schuyler and others that he and leaders in Congress favored Vermont's independence, which raised false hopes since New York and other states in Congress had lined up against Vermont's statehood.

Allen and others immediately rode to the Congress in Philadelphia again to appeal for statehood on Vermont's behalf. Traveling from Sunderland to Salisbury, Connecticut was a relatively quick and easy few days down the Battenkill, Hoosic, and Housatonic Rivers. But a ten-day ride to Philadelphia was much more time-intensive and hazardous. The time commitment Ethan spent lobbying Congress for statehood, not to mention his constant travel in and out of Vermont, is impressive. During the next few years, Ethan traveled to Connecticut, Boston,

Poughkeepsie, and other cities, trying to use his influence in the quest for Vermont's acceptance into the union.[7,8]

While the Allens and other Vermonters were growing their independent republic from the ground up, the Revolutionary War dragged on in the middle and southern colonies. The French joined the Patriot cause. By 1780, French King Louis XVI approved an expedition and transported troops to station in the U.S. He promoted Jean Baptiste Rochambeau to Lt. General and put him in command of French forces in America. On July 11, Comte de Rochambeau arrived in Newport, Rhode Island with a fleet of 450 officers and 5,300 French troops.

Battles against the British Army continued, with British victories in South Carolina at Charleston, Waxhaus, Camden, Guilford Courthouse, North Carolina, and Green Spring, Virginia. Vermont was vulnerable to invasion by a large British force to the north without being a recognized colony or having military protection. Vermont's vulnerability was concerning to the leaders and inhabitants of towns.

At the direction of the governor's council, Ethan continued to work as a political operative on Vermont's behalf. He began negotiating with former Green Mountain Boy Justus Sherwood, who had become a British secret agent at the war's outset. Sherwood was working for Governor General Frederick Haldimand, the commander of British forces in Montreal. Sherwood built a "Loyal Blockhouse" on North Hero Island. In 1780, the blockhouse became the headquarters for his spy network. Sherwood and Allen met at the blockhouse in Castleton and Arlington, the Loyal Blockhouse in North Hero, and other locations.

Even though the British northern army surrendered at Saratoga in 1777, they retreated to Montreal and still controlled the lake. Thousands of troops were entrenched there with accessible land and lake entry into Vermont. Devastating raids, killings, and kidnappings were still a threat to Vermonters. Modern historians should remember that in 1780, Vermont's leadership was very concerned about devastating British-led raids, similar to those repeated raids in Neshobe (Brandon) and Carleton's "slash and burn" raid that leveled villages from Middlebury to New Haven (Vergennes) and Panton, down Otter Creek to Lake

Champlain. In October 1780, Haldiman received a report from a British soldier in the Royalton raid:

"I burned twenty eight dwelling homes, thirty two barns full of grain, and one new barn, not quite finished, one saw mill and one grist mill, killed all the black cattle, sheep, pigs &c., which there was a great quantity. There was but very little hay. We burned close to a stockaded Fort, wherein there was a Captain and 60 men, but they could not turn out after us.... I got 32 prisoners and 4 scalps."[9,10]

During this time, Vermont was in a complex and challenging position. Thousands of the king's sailors and soldiers lived to the north with British warships on Lake Champlain. Congress was unwilling to admit Vermont as a state, provide armed forces, or protect the vulnerable Vermont territory from British-led raids. Vermont had only a part-time farmer militia of a few hundred Green Mountain Boys to defend itself. Even though the Revolutionary War battles had shifted to the middle and southern colonies, the settlers in many Vermont towns felt uncertain and at risk.

Sentiments of Vermonters regarding an alliance with Great Britain were polarized and fluid in some cases. Many Green Mountain Boys despised the "traitor" Justus Sherwood during the war. When Sherwood turned against the Patriot cause in 1776, the Boys ransacked his family's cabin in New Haven, Vermont. The Green Mountain Boys held a mock trial and sentenced Sherwood to life in confinement in the Simsbury, Connecticut, copper mine. Sherwood escaped from his captors and fled to the protection of the British at Crown Point, then north to Montreal.[11]

Settlers on the east side of Vermont, between the mountains and the Connecticut River, had been much more sympathetic to the British than settlers on the west side of the mountains. In negotiating with Sherwood, Allen had specific goals that overrode his feelings about Sherwood's treason. After multiple rejections for statehood by Congress, Vermont was in a challenging position. The question for the Allens, Governor Chittenden, Stephen Fay, and the rest of the governor's council was this: How could Vermont ensure security and promote economic success with an indifferent American government and a hostile British government across the border in Canada?

This replica of the 1781 British Loyal Block House was built around 1953 by Oscar E. Bredenberg of Champlain, New York. The North Hero Loyal Blockhouse was an outpost for British troops and spies from 1780 to 1795. *Vermont Historical Society, https://digitalvermont.org*

Allen's detractors quickly point out that he was a land speculator negotiating in the best interests of his family. However, northern Vermonters needed to trade potash, timber, and commodities outside the republic's boundaries. Vermonters depended on healthy trade with Canada to support Vermont's economy and stabilize and improve property values. Many Vermonters, especially in towns with access to the border, were interested in healthy trade with Canada and the stability and value of their land grants from New Hampshire.

Letters show that General Haldimand and Sherwood's spies ascertained that Vermonters would rather have the British army protect them than be attacked by them in raids. Since Congress was dragging its feet on granting Vermont statehood, correspondence shows that Sherwood and the British leadership calculated that Vermont might be amenable to becoming a British colony.[12]

With the authority of the Vermont Governor's Council, sometimes called the "Arlington Junto," including Governor Chittenden, Ethan, Ira, Stephen Fay, and a few others, Ethan negotiated a ceasefire to stop the British-led raids on Vermont villages. Second, with the backing of the Junto, Chittenden and Ethan negotiated a prisoner release, which freed hundreds of prisoners (including Green Mountain Boys) who had been captured in Vermont raids and military battles and taken to Canada to become enslaved or serve as indentured servants. Third, Allen wanted to ramp up pressure on Congress for admission to the union.

However, there was political blowback from Vermont to Valley Forge for Vermont negotiating with the British. Any affection General Washington had felt for Ethan was fading over concern about Allen's unendorsed negotiations with the British. Although some American generals wanted to arrest or even kidnap Allen, and the British wanted to kidnap him as well, Washington decided to give him a longer leash. But in the Vermont assembly, Ethan, appointed commander of the Vermont Militia, was accused of treason by several members. He promptly angrily resigned his appointment. Although Ethan bowed out of the lead role, the negotiations with Sherwood proceeded in 1781. For the next few years, Ira and Stephen Fay took over diplomatic duties for Vermont.[13]

At 30, on May 1, 1781, Ira Allen traveled from Sunderland to Isle Aux Noix on the Richelieu River with 19 militiamen. They arrived a week later. According to Sherwood's exasperated letters to Haldimand, Allen stalled on committing to a British alliance. Sherwood demanded Vermont become a British province. Negotiations continued for two weeks. Ira was cagey and evasive, concluding that he would need to get approval from Vermonters to make a deal. He briefed the Governor's Council the following month and was concerned about his safety due to tensions in negotiations. The British had also discussed kidnapping the Allens and successfully kidnapped other Vermont leaders. In July, the council signed a "Certificate for the Protection of Colonel Ira Allen." On August 4, Ira, Jonas Fay, and Bezaleel Woodward (from Dresden, New Hampshire) met with Congress again in Philadelphia.

Allen and his brothers, merchants Levi and Ira, and many other Vermonters were eager to improve British trade and end the war. Letters between British Governor General Haldiman and Justus Sherwood show the British eventually concluded, after several years of Stephen Fay and Ira Allen stalling an actual Vermont-British alliance, that the Vermonters were not serious about becoming a British Colony. The Vermonters had ulterior motives.[14]

Persistent attempts for Vermont's statehood continued for years to no avail. On February 1, 1780, Ira Allen, Jonas Fay, Stephen Rowe Bradley, and Moses Robinson appealed for Vermont statehood again in Philadelphia. Ethan was on the road, too.

"Reason" and the Beech Seal

In 1781, Ethan visited Dr. Young's widow, and she gave him their philosophical notes and probably a working manuscript from the work they had done in earlier years. Some Allen historians from his time and even today speculated that Young might have drafted and written some of the book. Young's biographers say Allen and Young co-authored *Reason the Only Oracle of Man* (*Reason*), which they had worked on since 1762. Although Allen didn't acknowledge Young's work on the book, the fact is, he didn't need to, based on practice and laws at the time.[15]

Plagiarism was not an ethical consideration during the 1780 American colonies and wasn't illegal, especially in Vermont, until after 1790. The vindication of plagiarism did not dampen the rage from the contemporary clergy about Allen's criticism of the church. Still, it does nullify the plagiarism accusations that some pundits made.[16]

In July 1782, Allen had finished his book, *Reason*, and approached printers Watson & Goodwin in Hartford, Connecticut about printing it. Allen was bullish about the potential for a good return on his heart-felt, long-anticipated writing project with Dr. Young that had begun two decades before. However, the publishers were more realistic and concerned about the public reaction to the book in the heavily Calvinist colony and stalled the printing project. Not to mention that Allen didn't have money to bankroll the printing at the time. His new book would have to wait while he tried to hustle donors to fund it.[17]

1783 was a big year for the United States and the Allen family. After the British surrender at Yorktown on October 19, 1782, a preliminary peace treaty was signed in Paris the following January. King George III issued a Proclamation of Cessation of Hostilities on February 4, and the Second Treaty of Paris was signed in September. It must have been an exciting time to be an American Patriot. But all was not well for the Allens.

In 1783, Ethan's daughter Loraine and wife Mary Brownson Allen passed away in Sunderland. This event marked a momentous shift in his life and the lives of his remaining daughters Mary Ann, Lucy Caroline, and toddler Pamela. Mary's death didn't slow Ethan down. In December of that year, Ethan was involved in a violent assault near his home. This story emerged almost 100 years later when an Ethan Allen memorial movement arose during the 1850s.

The report was published in the Burlington Free Press in 1889 by Dr. H. O. Bartlett of Milton. Bartlett's grandfather was Sunderland Constable Elisha Bartlett, who arrested General Ethan Allen on a complaint of assault. The complaint claimed that on December 2, 1783, Samuel Lucas and Allen had "high words," which led to an altercation in which Lucas raised the cane he carried. Lucas, a medium-sized man, threatened Allen, who was much bigger and more intimidating. Allen swiped the cane and "applied the 'Beach seal' to him so effectually that he was disabled for some days." When Lucas was able, he went to the Justice of the Peace Eli Pettibone, who issued a writ to Allen. Justice Pettibone passed the writ to Constable Bartlett, who served papers on General Allen. Allen anticipated the writ and responded by saying, "Got it, Elisha?" When Bartlett affirmed it, Allen replied, "Let's hear it roar."[18]

All parties appeared at the trial, but Allen asked for and was granted a continuance. Justice Pettibone made a record on the back of the writ and handed the document to Constable Bartlett, who took it home and locked it in a trunk at his home. Constable Bartlett then discovered he had important business in the state of New York, which he attended to but did not return until the day after Allen's trial resumed. When Bartlett returned, he found that all had participated in the court, but having no writ, there was no trial, "and all dispersed with great merriment."[19]

A year or more later, Allen appeared at Constable Bartlett's door at night. Allen asked, "Are you Elisha Bartlett, the constable of Sunderland, who took the body of Gen. Ethan Allen on a body writ?" "Yes." "Have you been paid for that service?" "No."[20]

Allen handed Bartlett a package. "There, take that. I guess it 'twill just about pay you. By the Eternal no man shall take the body of Ethan Allen and not have his pay."[21]

Inside the package was a fine piece of broadcloth. Allen had just returned from New York, and there, he had purchased enough cloth for a fine suit for himself and the constable. According to Dr. Bartlett's 1889 newspaper article, Dr. Bartlett had presented the yellowed writ at a then-recent Vermont Sons of the American Revolution meeting in Milton. Unfortunately, no court records corroborated this story nor did the original writ survive. Dr. H. O. Bartlett is listed as a member of the Sons of the American Revolution from Milton. Elisha Bartlett is listed as a Revolutionary War soldier on the Connecticut Rolls in the 1910 *Yearbook and Roster of the Society of the Sons of the American Revolution.*

In 1784, Allen took his manuscript to Haswell & Russell, printers in Bennington, hoping to print 1500 copies. He approached old acquaintances for loans, called in some debts, and pulled together over 1,000 pounds, mostly in credit, to pay his friend Anthony Haswell for printing *Reason* in Bennington. Folklore has it that a fire at the print shop burned all but a few hundred copies of the book. At any rate, the book never saw wide circulation during Allen's lifetime.[22]

That year, Allen was still active in Vermont politics, meeting with the Vermont assembly, continuing land speculation, and working with his attorney, Stephen Rowe Bradley, in Westminster. It is unlikely Ethan's remaining daughters, Lucy Caroline, 16; Mary Ann, 12; and Pamela, five, were capable of fending for themselves and running the household once Mary was gone. It might not have been a safe or ideal scenario. The tight-knit Allen family continued the pattern of supporting each other.

Ethan's brother Heman had housed Mary and the family for years, then Zimri housed them in Sheffield, Massachusetts, before they moved to Vermont. Uncle Ira also had a history of sheltering Heman and Heber's widows and their children and even educating them through college. Mary's family, the Brownsons, also lived nearby in Sunderland. We don't know if Ethan's girls immediately found different accommodations with the Brownsons or Ira when Mary became ill and died or if they stayed put in their Sunderland home fending for themselves during the months following Mary's death. As it would turn out, a different family adventure awaited them shortly.[23]

11

Fanny Montresor Brush
Buchanan 1760 - 1834

Fanny Montresor Brush portrait, painted
when she was 11, the year she moved to
Westminster, Vermont.
Public domain

Fanny Montresor was born out of wedlock in 1760 to British officer Captain John Montresor and a mother who died during or shortly after childbirth. Fanny's Aunt Margaret raised her in New York City. In 1762, Margaret married Crean Brush, who happened to be one of the high-profile "Yorkers," despised by the Green Mountain Boys. Brush was an Irish immigrant, an educated attorney with extravagant taste in apparel and his family's furnishings. A January 1772 invoice from New York clothier Adam Gilchrist shows Brush bought yards of silk, dimity pockets, scarlet fabrics, vests, satin garters for breeches, and gold lace.

Fanny enjoyed an affluent lifestyle while growing up in New York City's polite society before the war and became accustomed to the finer things in life. She was educated in the classics, spoke fluent French, played the lute and guitar, read voraciously, studied botany, and lived fashionably. In 1771, when she was 11, her family moved to the poshest home in Westminster. The young Fanny Brush was a novelty in the oldest town in Vermont and bloomed into a "clever gentlewoman."[1]

As a teen, Fanny lost her soldier fiancé, who drowned in a river. Then, Fanny married Captain John Buchanan of the British Navy. Fanny's first marriage at 16 is said to have been arranged by her stepfather, Crean Brush, so she could live with the supervision and protection of Buchanan's family when he was away on military service. Buchanan died in battle shortly after they married. Folklore has it that they produced a son who passed away, although there is no tangible record. Fanny's stepfather, Crean Brush, was a significant person in Vermont for more than one reason.

Brush worked closely with several New York governors and became a New York assemblyman. When New York sheriffs and posses were intimidated and sent packing by the Green Mountain Boys, Mr. Brush suggested putting a bounty on Ethan Allen's head, which New York did. New York also targeted several other Green Mountain Boys officers with bounties.

Allen responded to the bounties by publishing a reward for two New York officials and insultingly putting a much smaller bounty on their heads. In response to then-Assemblyman Crean Brush and Samuel Wells, Allen called them "busie understrappers to a Number of More Overgrown Villains... The Green Mountain Boys will not Fairly resign their Necks to the Halter to be Hang'd by your Curst Fraternity of Land Jockeys who would Better Adorn a Halter than we." Allen mentioned, "visiting your abode," and publicly invited Brush to the Catamount Tavern, where the Green Mountain Boys would acquaint him with the "beech seal" (i.e., give him a whipping).[2]

Brush died in 1778, and two conflicting accounts describe his violent demise. In one scenario, he committed suicide with a pistol. But a witness affidavit says Brush's throat had been cut with a straight razor while he was working alone in a Manhattan law office. New York had ostracized Brush after raiding Patriot property in Boston and serving prison time. He was disgraced and had lost a lot of his fortune. Suicide was a plausible scenario. But historians John Duffy and Nicholas Muller postulated that Ethan Allen committed the murder. At the time, Allen was on parole but under British guard, living nearby in the low-security New York Provost Jail. Could Allen have managed to slip out of his confinement, travel from the jail to the law office, kill Brush, and slip back into his jail undetected? At this point, we don't know who possessed the lethal hand. There were no suspects, and no one was charged with the crime. On another interesting side note, Brush's Loyalist Westminster attorney, John Grout, whom the Green Mountain Boys had sent packing to Canada during the war, "disappeared" at about the same time. Nothing is known of Grout's fate.[3,4]

Brush's will split his 60,000-acre Vermont estate three ways. His heirs included his wife Margaret, his daughter Elizabeth, who still lived in Ireland, and his stepdaughter Fanny. Unfortunately, Vermont confiscated and sold his estate, and it wouldn't be easy for his heirs to get it back. The confiscation and sale of their home forced Margaret and Fanny to live in Boston with Margaret's second husband, Patrick Wall, whom Margaret had married in 1780. When Margaret and Fanny returned to Westminster to recover the Brush estate, they rented a room at Bradley's boarding house. Serendipitously, an October 1783 invoice shows that Ethan Allen previously stayed at Bradley's inn, ate 56 meals, and ran a "liquor" tab for eighteen nights.[5,6]

The 46-year-old General Ethan Allen wasn't shy about wearing his impressive dress military uniform and regalia in public. At some point, the Vermont celebrity met the beautiful, charming, educated, clever 24-year-old gentlewoman, Frances Montresor Brush, known as Fanny. If anyone could reverse the Brush heirs' property misfortunes, it would have been the influential and ever-zealous General Ethan Allen. He regularly appeared at the courthouse or legislative meetings in Westminster, and he and Fanny likely met in the bustling town or at Bradley's boarding house.

Most of Fanny's story comes from 20th-century Ethan Allen

biographers such as Brown, Holbrook, Jellison, and other historians whose accounts sometimes conflict and only sporadically cite their sources. In some cases, the traditional folklore is inaccurate, and this book cites primary sources whenever possible.

Folklore says Fanny sang and played the guitar by the fireplace after dinner at the Bradley house. Another legend comes from a tavern owner named John Norton teasing Fanny with speculation of marrying the widower Allen and becoming a queen of Vermont. Fanny replied that if she married the Devil, she would be Queen of Hell. Whether this conversation happened or not is up for debate. Regardless of the validity, it is interesting that Norton considered General Allen a king of Vermont in the story. If Allen had royal status among Vermonters, it would give credence to his celebrity during his life, despite those who believe his status was inflated in the 1850s.[7]

Stephen Rowe Bradley's son, William Czar Bradley, was the first to write the prevailing and widely repeated marriage tale of Fanny and Ethan. The story goes that Ethan strolled into Stephen Rowe Bradley's dining room and greeted the Supreme Court justices sitting around the table at Bradley's inn. They offered Allen breakfast. Allen declined, walked into the next room, caught Fanny off guard, and said, "Fanny, if we are ever going to marry, now is the time."

The two walked out into the dining room. After ensuring they were committed to their momentous decision, Ethan's old friend, Chief Justice Moses Robinson, officiated the vows, and the couple married on the spot. After Fanny threw together a bag and grabbed her guitar and a coat, they dashed away on a sleigh, heading toward Bennington with Allen's servant at the reins.

Some historians consider this story historical fiction since it is based on second-hand folklore passed down a generation. The source of the wedding story, William Czar Bradley (1782-1867), was just two years old on their wedding day. Whatever the circumstances or duration of the courtship, we know the two were married on February 9th.

On February 21, 1784, the (Bennington) *Vermont Gazette* published a brief marriage announcement. After meeting Fanny, Ethan's friend Anthony Haswell wrote a wedding announcement, naming her Lydia, possibly to disguise her name to avoid questions about her identity as the stepdaughter of the despised Crean Brush:

"Married. at Westminster, on Monday the 9th inst. The Hon. General ETHAN ALLEN, to the amiable Mrs. LYDIA BUCHANAN. A lady possessing in an eminent degree, every graceful qualification requisite to render the Hymenial bands felicitous."[8]

Although some biographers play up a romantic angle to the relationship, another plausible reason for Fanny's interest in Ethan was her mission to recover her inheritance, the grand Brush estate. According to documents from attorney Udney Hay, Ethan provided a $500 marriage bond to Fanny. Ethan was the best option at the time to add momentum to their efforts, particularly since he would have had a personal stake in Fanny's property, given the couverture laws that favored husbands. The fact that Fanny's stepfather was Crean Brush may have aroused some mystique for the widower Allen. As was standard then, Ethan needed a mother for his girls, a partner to run his household, and a mother to bear more Allen children. In his world, that role would become Fanny's duty. Recovering Fanny's inheritance became Ethan's duty, and he approached it zealously.

Whatever their possible interests, we know that Fanny and Ethan married and relocated to Sunderland and possibly Bennington. Some biographers say they quickly moved 20 miles south to a rented house in the more cosmopolitan town of Bennington for the next few years. If the newlyweds lived in the Allen Homestead in the thriving community in the Arlington-Sunderland area, they would have been in the nucleus of Vermont's government.

Governor Thomas Chittenden ran Vermont from his home in Arlington. Just up the road in Sunderland, Ira Allen was Vermont Surveyor General and Treasurer next door to Ethan; Matthew Lyon, a future U.S. senator, served as Ira's assistant. The Brownson family ran a tavern and store and lived close by, along with other prominent Vermonters who lived in the now prominent community.

Scarce primary source material reveals Fanny's relationship with

Lucy Caroline, Mary Ann, and Pamela, the three Allen girls. Fanny grew up in a Loyalist household in relative luxury and was possibly accustomed to having servants and modern conveniences. The Allen girls had grown up above Uncle Heman's store and on farms in Sheffield and Sunderland. They grew up living close to the harshness and challenges of nature. There may have been a cultural, socioeconomic, or personality divide or rift between Fanny and the girls. The four of them lived together in close quarters for three years in the Sunderland-Bennington area, then another two years in Burlington.

The following October, after the 1784 marriage, Fanny delivered a baby girl named Frances (Fanny) Margaret Allen in Sunderland. Fanny Margaret would grow up to eclipse her mother's name recognition. They continued to live there, with Ethan often away, before relocating to the frontier community of Burlington in 1787.[9]

By the mid-1780s, northern Vermont was changing. Green Mountain Boy war hero and fourth-cousin Colonel Ebenezer Allen had built a comfortable cabin and farm on the southern tip of the southernmost island of Two Heroes in Lake Champlain, a few miles north of the Onion River. The island settlement had mushroomed into a town of several hundred inhabitants, and Ebenezer was the town clerk and soon-to-be innkeeper. Ethan's brother Ira had found a choice spot on the Onion River bordering Colchester and Burlington, and the Onion River Land Company owned tens of thousands of acres on both river banks and on the east side of Lake Champlain in Burlington, Shelburne, Charlotte, to name a few. Ira was building mills, and permanent settlements sprouted on Colchester and Burlington's north and south river banks.

In Burlington, several families had built farms near the river, and several more built cabins on the bay near the lake. Burlington sat on a hillside forest facing the lake highway and the Adirondack Mountains, bordered by the Onion River to the north. It had massive potential for growth and development. Ira had purchased several hundred acres on the river for Ethan in 1778. With sawmills coming soon to the river and the area seeing a steady influx of new Vermonters, Burlington looked like the land of opportunity.

What lifestyle did Fanny enjoy in Sunderland and Bennington, and what family dynamics prevailed for those few years? Did the girls offer help with the new baby, Fanny Margaret? Did Fanny Allen have housekeeping help from servants? What did Fanny envision for the future, and did she have occasion to preview the Allen homestead in Burlington and consider the adaptations she would need to make before moving?

12

The End of The Onion River Land Company and Beginning of the Frontier Farm Life 1785-1787

While Fanny managed the home life, Ethan was still actively buying and selling land during the mid-1780s, even as he was considering dissolving the Onion River Land Company (ORLC) with Ira and eyeing a move to a quieter farm life in Burlington. He felt a sense of accomplishment with the extraordinary popularity of his first book, *A narrative of Col. Ethan Allen's captivity....* When his book, *Reason the Only Oracle of Man... (Reason)*, finally began a print run at Anthony Haswell's press in Bennington, Ethan inscribed his first copy of *Reason* to Fanny:

"Dear Fanny wise, the beautiful and young, The partner of my Joys, my dearest self, My life, pride of my life, your sexes pride, And pattern of sincere politeness, To thee a welcome compliment I make Of treasures rich, the oracles of reason." Unlike his first book, the narrative of his captivity, *Reason* sold very few copies and drew condemnation from critics as soon as it was in circulation. Nonetheless, he promoted it widely to his friends and acquaintances.[1]

Moving from the Sunderland-Bennington area to Burlington would've been a formidable journey and change for the Allens. The Sunderland/Bennington area teemed with thousands of people; Bennington alone had 2,400 residents, with well-established taverns, stores, mills, and roads. But the Allens still had dreams of their cherished Onion River forever home.

Ira had surveyed, claimed, bought, and explored the area he called the "Burlington Pine Plain" since the early 1770s. By 1785, Burlington was still a forested frontier town with around a hundred residents. The beginning of a settlement had remained dormant throughout the war, with only a few people brave and adventurous enough to set down roots. Burlington was still a dense forest of seemingly unlimited timber, fertile soils, and waterways for shipping on the lake and river, with the promise of future settlers demanding land and resources.

In direct conflict with the ORLC, New York believed it owned all of the Grants, now known as Vermont. Ira was familiar with several New York surveyors, such as William Cockburn, John Stevens, and William Blanchard, who surveyed most of Vermont as early as 1772. New York survey maps, including Onion River; Lamoille River; Otter Creek; Socialborough, a 1771 New York town in the Pittsford-Rutland area; Halesborough (Brandon); and other towns dating to the early 1770s reside in the New York State Library. Referring to the survey map on the adjacent page, Cockburn wrote, "There was intervale very good & very large, as large as large as I ever saw. From the Mouth of the Lemoil River toward the Point of Land near the Mouth of Onion River then along the Bank of the Lake."

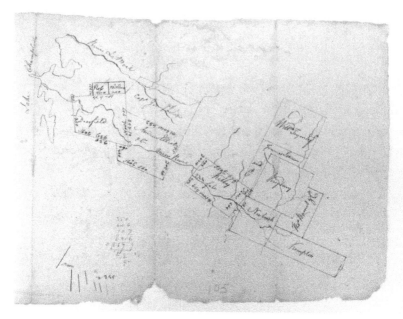

A 1772 New York map of the Onion and Lamoille Rivers and nearby lands. It resides in the William Cockburn files and may have been created by William Blanchard. Note Lake Champlain on the left. Deerfield is the New York town that was earlier chartered by New Hampshire as Burlington.
NYS Libraries, Gary Shattuck.

The ORLC on the Burlington Pine Plain

The earliest European settler in Burlington was Felix Powell, from Dorset, Vermont, originally from Connecticut. He bought two New Hampshire Grants lots on what is now Appletree Point and a couple of others on the river, lots 32 and 33. These lots now comprise the Ethan Allen Homestead, where the Ethan Allen house and Brownell Education Center sit today. Powell or one of his associates may have cleared and farmed some of the homestead lands for a couple of years. He and other nearby early settlers at the falls in Colchester near Ira's blockhouse left their Burlington area land ahead of the Redcoat raids in 1775. They retreated south for a few years until the Northern British Army surrendered at Saratoga in 1777. [2]

Powell sold his Burlington properties shortly after he left and sold the intervale lots on the river to William Marsh, a Loyalist. The Vermont republic confiscated and sold Marsh's land in 1778, along with other Loyalist land. Ira first suggested that Vermont fund the militia by seizing and selling Loyalist properties in the Grants. The Governor's Council and Vermont Assembly liked the idea, and the fledgling republic adopted that policy. Tens of thousands of acres were confiscated and resold during the 1770s. [3]

Ira stepped in and bought the William Marsh lots on behalf of Ethan, which included about 300 acres of high and dry land on a sandy plateau above the meandering river, from Colonel James Claghorn, the Commissioner of the Confiscation and Sale of the Estates of Vermont and the United States in 1778.[4]

The ORLC began in 1772 as an "all for one and one for all" real estate operation. The partners started with their hard-earned savings from their labors or money from selling the Allen family farm in Cornwall. By 1778, Ira and Ethan were the surviving partners. Although Levi was not officially a partner, deeds show he bought and sold land for the ORLC.

The land speculation strategy was to buy, improve, subdivide, and sell at a profit. The improved land was called a "pitch." In some cases, squatters moved onto vacant land, hoping that an absentee owner would forget about it or relinquish it by not paying taxes. When we look at the deeds and court records about the Ethan Allen homestead, it is clear that pitching by squatters occurred over the years on the intervale. This practice, and the fact that the present Ethan Allen Homestead Park includes several hundred-acre parcels, makes understanding exactly what happened, who owned what, and when challenging.

Speculators who bought land often built a shanty or rudimentary cabin and perhaps cleared an acre or two each year on their "pitch," which would constitute the beginning of a farm. They could sell the lots for more than the purchase price. Large lots of 300 to 500 acres were bought as "rights," then subdivided into smaller parcels, and resold after they appreciated over time. Then, the speculator could use the profits to buy and sell more land. The first rule of real estate was and still is "location, location, location." The second rule was, "Buy low, sell high." Unfortunately for land speculators, the second rule was more difficult to accomplish, but the Allens figured they had the ideal location on the Onion River.

From his home in Sunderland, Vermont, in 1785, Ethan penned a note to Ira in Colchester and asked his brother to build a 34-by-24-foot farmhouse on his land on the Burlington side of Onion River. Ethan had plans to move his family there and pursue a quiet farming life. Ira followed through and found two men, Josiah Averil and Jon Butterfield, to build a house in 1785 on the river lots Ira had purchased on Ethan's behalf. Averil and Butterfield were to improve and farm the land on "General Allen's land" on the intervale by the river in Burlington one year at a time.[5]

At that time, Ira was land-rich but cash-strapped. Nevertheless, he built two river mills to grind wheat and saw lumber. By the mid-1780s, Ira, cousin Ebenezer Allen, and others were shipping logs and beef down the lake into the Richelieu River in Canada. Brother Levi operated a store on the Richelieu in St. John, Quebec. As a merchant, Levi sold goods and obtained British sundries via Canada for Ira's store in Burlington. The Burlington lumber added a new dimension to the business and provided beams and planks for local buildings.

But Levi's location in St. John, Quebec was a relatively small trading port. The Allens wanted to sell their goods directly to buyers in Montreal, Quebec; Halifax, Nova Scotia; and, in time, to Europe. To do that they would need to build a canal around the rapids just north of St. John to get to the mighty St Lawrence River and out to the Atlantic Ocean. The Allens expected the Burlington mills to anchor development in the Champlain Valley and produce lumber and grain for international trade.

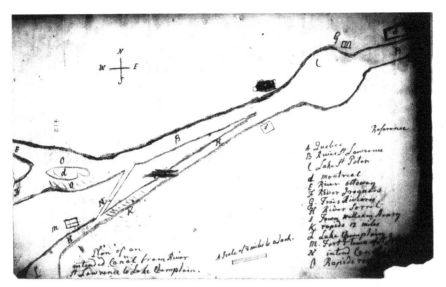

Remember Baker's son, 17-year-old Ozi Baker, sent this Richelieu River map depicting a proposed canal built around the rapids to Ira Allen in 1778.
Stevens Collection microfilm, UVM Silver Special Collections.

In 1778, 17-year-old Ozi Baker, Remember Baker's son, sent Ira Allen a "Plan of a canal from the River St Lawrence to Lake Champlain" on the Richelieu River to circumvent the dangerous shoals, which were obstacles to shipping downriver toward Montreal and the Atlantic Ocean. Pursuing a canal, a monumental engineering and financial project, would become a never-realized goal of the Allens. Unfortunately, the canal was not built until the 1830s, long after the pioneer Allen generation was gone.[6]

In October 1786, the Vermont Governor's Council commissioned Levi Allen to negotiate a trade treaty with Quebec. After much negotiation, Lord Dorchester (Guy Carleton) granted a trade agreement to Vermont in 1787. Ira Allen's mills were cutting lumber at the falls on the Onion River, and they already had lumber customers in St. John, Quebec.

Even without the canal, the Allens predicted better profits if they could work directly with Great Britain. There seemed to be no end to the old-growth timber supply in Vermont, and Great Britain would be a vast market for lumber, masts, and potash. Levi continued his mercantile business with a trading post in St. John. For years, he bought Canadian and British goods to supply Ira's store on the river in Burlington. The Allens' business practice was to borrow on credit, speculate land, cut local timber, saw timber into milled lumber, sell lumber and potash to Canada, and import finished goods for local settlers. Although Burlington consisted of a handful of buildings on the bay, a small settlement on the river, and a few more homes scattered across the forest, new settlers were coming to Burlington.

Ethan continued to sell parcels, call in his debts, and settle his accounts to prepare for moving the family to Burlington. He owed a small debt of 14 pounds to Libeus Armstrong of Bennington, who had extended Ethan's credit. By the end of the year, Armstrong had enlisted an attorney, Ethan's future son-in-law Samuel Hitchcock, to force Ethan to pay up.

In a telling move in January 1787, Ethan wrote a letter to his brother Levi. He described his problem and implored Levi to "exert yourself to the utmost skill" to convince "little" Armstrong to drop the debt against him. We don't know if or how Levi resolved the situation. We know from recorded anecdotes that Levi had succeeded in discharging other debts by cursing and threatening to kill people.[7]

Ira had leased the future Ethan Allen homestead lots to two tenant farmers named Josiah Averil and Thomas Butterfield for at least two years. After building a house on the property in 1785, the two men continued to improve and farm the lots again during 1786. The contract with Ira included growing peas, oats, wheat, and corn. The early farmers likely had cut down any trees near the house, and the river was a wide meandering vista from the house.[8]

Averill and Butterfield agreed to farm and improve the land, build fencing, and leave produce for Ethan when they vacated in the spring of 1787 so "General Allen" could move in. But only some things were going according to plan for Ira. James Hawley, whom Ira had contracted with to run his mills at Onion River, wrote to Ira on March 28, 1787, to inform him that floods at the dam had destroyed the mill on the Onion

River. Everything was gone. Ira was still in Sunderland until May, and the mill and dam infrastructure repairs would take time.[9]

The Allens depended on the revenues from their products to purchase goods for their stores in St. John and on the river. The flooding temporarily slowed cash flow and the Allens' real estate, lumber, and other mercantile businesses. At one point, Levi and Ira lamented that they needed a revenue source since they had significant expenses after buying large quantities of store stock from London and had no success selling lumber in return.

Unfortunately, the sluggish post-war economy, a lack of cash, and longer-term maturity horizons in land assets, not to mention the illiquidity of real estate and perhaps unrealistic expectations, all conspired to make ORLC profitability a very long-horizon proposition. And there was one other factor if those weren't enough. Most of the ORLC partners, including Remember Baker, Zimri Allen, and Heman Allen, had died by 1778, leaving only Ethan and Ira. Levi played an essential role in buying and selling Vermont properties, but technically, he was never one of the original partners. Now that the rest were gone, the three remaining brothers relied on each other as much as ever. Now that the ORLC was ending, Ethan contacted old friends with unfinished diplomatic business. One friend was Hector St. John de Crevecoeur, a former cartographer for the French militia in the French and Indian War.

De Crevecoeur, who later changed his name to an Americanized Hector St. John, had stayed in New York after the war. He was a philosopher and wrote a book titled *Letters From an American Farmer*, which encapsulated his Patriot-friendly views and living the American dream. His book became popular in his home country when he translated it into French. Upon traveling home, he was appointed French Consul to America. He met a woman named Mehitable Tippet. Tippet and St. John married, settled on a farm in Chester, New York, and raised a family.[10]

On April 4, 1787, Ethan sent a letter to his friend, St. John. Ethan followed through on what he called American feelings of "honorable and worthy patriotism of France" to the American war cause. Allen worked with Vermont leadership to bestow naturalized Vermont citizenship to St. John's three sons. Allen also proclaimed a new one-mile square city of "Vergennesburg," in New Haven, named St. Johnsbury and Danville, to honor France. Allen sent his friend a copy of his book, *Reason*, to be shared with the Academy of Arts and Sciences in Paris, and "by whose Sentence I expect to Stand or fall." In 1789, St. John was admitted to the American Philosophical Society and, in Paris, the Society of the Friends of the Blacks, an abolitionist organization.[11]

In Burlington, Allen was gearing up for the farm business. On May 1, 1787, Ira signed a promissory note to Ethan for 50 pounds of neat cattle, due in 14 months. This note and other letters confirm that the Allens were raising and selling cattle to Canada, which was timely since brother Levi had just gotten the British to open trade between Vermont and Canada.

More importantly, Ethan and Ira officially dissolved the ORLC on that date. According to the agreement, Ethan kept 400 acres and his farm buildings and gave up all of the mill sites and intervale river lots, except for the ones Ira specifically gave him. Ira relinquished lots 33 and 34, the two lots west of 32 and 33, which is the site of the present Ethan Allen house and visitor center museum. Ethan gained his deceased partner Heman Allen's 1,000 acres of land contiguous to Burlington Bay, and the agreement stated that Ira had already paid state taxes on that land.

In addition, the agreement stipulated that Ira would: "build a house and other buildings for sd. Ethan in the vicinity of Onion River as soon as Planks can be conveniently sawed at said Ira's mills and seasoned fit for you in such a form or fashion as sd. Ethan will give instructions for to the value or expense of five hundred pounds in lawful money."

The agreement also committed Ira to pay Ethan one hundred pounds in goods at Ira's store near Onion River at the market price on the first day of August for the following seven years. It gave Ethan a deed to one thousand choice acres near Lake Memphremagog as soon as it could be surveyed.[12]

Although Ethan and Ira officially dissolved the ORLC, Ira and Levi worked as a team to push trade with Canada and the British. Ira would later trust Levi enough to sign over a power of attorney when he sailed to London to lobby for a canal and buy weapons. But the future success of their real estate and mercantile ventures would take some patience. The sluggish economy didn't help attract new settlers to the northern half of Vermont and kept land appreciation stagnant.

By the spring of 1787, Ethan was finalizing preparations to move his family to the Burlington farm. Letters show he was in Burlington in May and June. Ethan wrote a letter from Burlington to Levi in St. John, saying there was no flour in Vermont, and they sorely needed wheat. He asked Levi to return wheat or flour with Mr. McLean, who had delivered his letter. Ethan commented that his farming business was brisk and, "I hear my family is well."[13]

We can assume Fanny and the Allen sisters were still in Sunderland or Bennington most of that summer, and all was well, based on Ethan's comment to Levi. But only for a short time. An unusual growing season followed, with a cold, wet spring and dry summer. In June, there was no grain to harvest. Farmers would only have one wheat harvest. The uncooperative weather postponed the flour milling till late summer at best. A letter from Ira to Levi later in the month echoed Ethan's concern—flour was scarce, and there was no bread without flour. But the real estate market was the Allens' big concern.

On May 9, 1787, the *Vermont Gazette* ran an announcement titled "Encouragement for Settling on Onion River." It promoted outstanding land for sale in Burlington, Colchester, and St Albans "owned by gentlemen who wish to facilitate settlement of the country." They offered "lease to own" terms, free rail fences on high-yield soils near the river, accessible lake and logging port access, and free trade with Canada to the north. The ads envisioned opportunities "to point Onion River and its vicinity as a future place of grandeur, covered with flourishing and extensive settlements." The following men signed the advertisement: Ira Allen, Frederick Saxton, Dubartus Willand, John M'Lane, David Stanton, Solomon Cooley, Joel Woodworth, William Coit, and Thos. Butterfield. Within three years it would grow by hundreds of residents.

The Burlington Allen family was about to become one group of those new settlers.[14]

13

The Burlington Years
1787-1789

Seventeen eighty-seven was a hectic year for Ethan: promoting his book, working on recovering the Brush estate for Fanny, and preparing to move his family. He continued the real estate business with his two surviving brothers. Ira and Levi also operated general stores and sold lumber, logs, and other goods in their stores at Onion River Falls and St. John, Quebec, respectively. In particular, Levi sold shiploads of barrel staves and jockeyed to sell ship masts and spars to Canada and Great Britain.

Only a handful of houses existed on the Burlington Bay and another settlement at the falls on the Onion River. Early accounts note besides Felix Powell, Captain John Collins, Job Boynton, and Gideon King, Sr. had all built homes on Burlington Bay by the 1770s and mid-1780s. In addition, the small settlement on the river included a gristmill and a sawmill by 1786, and a few houses dotted the riverbanks and hillsides. The Allen friends, Stephen and Mary Lawrence, ran a farm near the high bridge a few miles upriver.[1,2]

One of those new arrivals to Burlington was Massachusetts native and Harvard graduate attorney Samuel Hitchcock, who arrived in 1786.

Hitchcock would soon meet and court Ethan and Mary's daughter, Lucy Caroline Allen. The two dated during the next couple of years while the Allen family lived in Burlington. They married in April 1789, two months after Ethan's death.[3]

In June, Ethan, Levi, and Ira visited Lord Dorchester (Guy Carleton, Governor General of the British forces in Canada) in Quebec City to lobby for selling and shipping beef to Canada. But the trading relationship was complicated, to put it mildly. British ships still roamed Lake Champlain, taxed cargo, and impressed (removed) sailors they deemed to be citizens of the United Kingdom. They also taxed or blocked cargo periodically. Even though the war had ended a few years before, there were diverging opinions within Canada on trade with Vermont. Any hopes of lasting free trade would be in flux for a few years.

To make it worse, merchants in Canada were demanding cash and not extending "notes" for debts with the Allens due to their lack of currency. Ethan was not directly involved in the mercantile business, but Ira and Levi owed Canadian merchants money for their imports. They sought to sell the lumber from the mill and use the credit to pay off bills for the London merchandise they had purchased. In more than one case, Canadian merchants refused to buy their lumber shipments because of low demand or because the Allens' product didn't meet their high standards. At one point, the Allens didn't have money to pay their men to bring their rejected lumber home, let alone they would have been traveling against the water current. After sitting out all winter in Canada, the lumber was checked and split and was worthless to sell by spring.[4]

Business at Levi's store was apparently profitable. Levi's wife Nancy and Prince were running the business that summer, with seven-year-old little Nancy. In June, Nancy, then 39, was taking a break and staying with her friend, Betsey Franks. The Nancys were visiting Montreal's Vauxhall Gardens, owned by John Franks, Betsey's father. Vauxhall was a Parisian-style "pleasure park" with amusements, music, and other entertainment.

On June 29, Nancy wrote a letter to Ethan from Montreal. She wrote in beautiful cursive penmanship. On this occasion, she reached out to Ethan for several reasons.

> "Montreal
>
> Dear Brother
>
> Have just time to inform you of your Brothers Safe arrival at Quebeck with the small quantity of lumber, he wrote me he had reason to believe Should be Successful, Wish to God he May, for repeated Misfortunes have almost turnd my brains... Am in great want my tables Chairs and bedsteds, Do be kind enough to get them made as Soon as possible, Suppose you have little time to Spare. Dare Say you have enough to do to take care of your business and your large Famely of Children for I hear you have at least one Dozen, Well done old rogue, Shall have but a poor opinion of you after this, I wish you a Spedy reformation.
>
> Nancy Allen"[5]

Notably absent in the letter was regard for Ethan's young wife, Fanny. Her reference to a speedy reformation indicates that Fanny and the children had not arrived in Burlington yet, as far as Nancy knew. Her playful tone suggests an amicable relationship between the two of them.

Nancy's note also suggests Ethan was responsible for making or having furniture made for Levi and Nancy. Woodworking skills were common among the settlers, but furniture-making was a craft. Ethan apparently had some responsibility for producing furniture for the family.

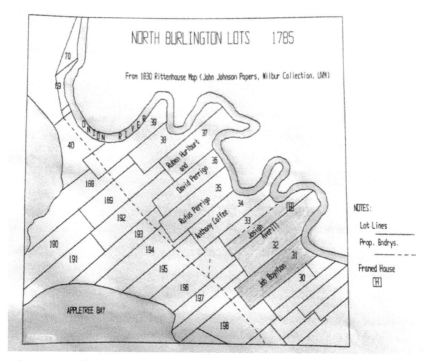

The 1785 map of Burlington shows the site of the Allen homestead on lots 32 and 33, farmed in that year by Averil and Butterfield.
UVM Special Collections

The next day, Ira penned a note to Levi mentioning he was still looking for wheat, and they were still repairing the flood damage at the mill, and he was "Disappointed about the furniture for Nancy & myself for the Present." We don't know if Ethan was overextended or if the mill flooding contributed to the lack of finished lumber for making furniture, or shipping it to Nancy in St. John.

Allen spent some time in Burlington during the spring and summer of 1787. We don't know the precise date when his family moved north, but it can be narrowed down to a window in August. On July 6th, Ira wrote to brother Levi that Ethan had purchased a boat that was "deficient of sales and cordage," to "move his family up." Ira asked if Levi could equip the boat for sailing up to Burlington.[6]

The Allens would have moved their possessions from Sunderland overland in oxcarts to the lake. The most likely land route leg of the trip could have been either the "Fair Haven Road" to Skenesboro or the Crown Point Military Road to Chimney Point. From either of those starting points for the water journey, with a good prevailing southerly tailwind, it would take at least a few more days of sailing and rowing to reach their new home in Burlington.

What was the most likely route if the Allen family moved to Burlington over water? Battenkill River guides say navigating that river in a boat larger than a per-

Map of the plausible route the Ethan Allen family took from Sunderland to Burlington in August 1787.
Google map

sonal watercraft would have been unlikely, if not impossible. Let alone the river doesn't connect with Lake Champlain. Allen likely would have docked his boat on the Vermont side near Skenesboro (Whitehall) or perhaps Chimney Point.

A sailboat could carry their worldly possessions over water to Burlington if they used an ox cart to get to the lake. Water travel with family possessions and livestock would have been far more economical and possibly faster than overland travel since the "path" from Sunderland to Burlington, particularly the section north of Middlebury, was virtually impassable for anything wider than an ox cart. And even then, rocks, stumps, marshland, and other obstacles would have made for a slow and jarring slog.

It would have been a 2-mile-per-hour walk, with oxen hauling family possessions in carts over roughly 100 miles of primitive rocky, stumpy, swampy paths. Traveling 10 miles daily on the oxcart would have been ambitious in the Champlain Valley. Either way, by land or water, the Allens would have been exposed to the elements and subject to the unpredictable weather. They would have stayed at inns for the weeks-long trek or longer if they extended the trip.

There are accounts of typical accommodations found at inns. In a Winooski Historical Society Group post, historian David Blow discovered an account of the Brownell Tavern in Colchester near the Onion River as an example. There was a central fireplace and chimney. A kitchen faced east and a sitting room faced the sunset. The upstairs was all one large room, with a dozen beds. Two or more people slept in a bed if necessary, when it was crowded. Latecomers would curl up in a corner on the floor.

Moving the family possessions during 1787 would have been an exciting ordeal but even more challenging because, by August, Fanny was six months into her pregnancy with Hannibal, their second child. Unlike today, where we enjoy a relatively accurate delivery date prediction and standard of care, 18th-century obstetrics was more of a guessing game. A drafty frame house in northern Vermont may not have seemed an ideal delivery room for birthing in the frosty Vermont autumn/winter. What was the solution?

A blacksmith named Captain John Collins ran an inn on Lake Street (now Battery Street), overlooking the bay, where the John Pomeroy House was later built and still stands today. The Collins Inn may not have had a maternity ward, but it was better than the small Allen house by the river. Henry Collins later recounted that the Allens stayed with them for three months until Franny delivered baby Hannibal on November 24, 1787. That time window would back-date the Allen family's arrival in Burlington to late August or early September.[7]

The Allen family now included Ethan (49); Fanny (27); Lucy Caroline (19); MaryAnn (15); Pamela (8) (from Ethan's first marriage to Mary Brownson); Ethan and Fanny's daughter Fanny Margaret (3), who had been born on October 24, 1784; and newborn Hannibal Montresor Allen. The household also likely included several of their workers.

Before or after his family's journey northward in August, Ethan wrote to Major Royall Tyler in Massachusetts during a stop in Bennington. Tyler had been called back into military service to help quell Shays' Rebellion, and had appealed to Allen for help in returning Shays to be prosecuted. In Allen's reply, he asked Tyler for support to publish his book's appendix, also known as *An essay on the universal plentitude of being....* Allen's note gives the impression that he had already completed the appendix and sought funding to publish it.

Even though Allen had a history of rebelling against the church and government authority, in the Tyler letter, Allen reassured Tyler of his lack of support for Daniel Shays and his insurrectionists, who were wanted in Massachusetts and seeking refuge in Vermont. Shays and his men had escaped to Vermont to avoid prosecution. Despite Major Tyler's effort to return Shays and his followers to justice in Massachusetts, including traveling to Vermont, the Vermont Legislature refused to support Tyler's wishes. However, Governor Chittenden wrote that Vermont would not shield Shays and his followers. Royall Tyler would later move to Guilford, then to Brattleboro, and become elected to the Vermont General Assembly, Windham County State's Attorney, and in 1801, the Vermont Supreme Court. Tyler was also a novelist and playwright of some prominence in the states. After some time in Vermont, cooler heads prevailed in Massachusetts, and Shays and his men vacated their Vermont settlement and went home.

> "Bennington, 28th August '87
> Sir,
> You will find by this time I dare say that the government of this State have been very friendly to yours, such criminals and person who have acted against the law and [so] society, in general and have came from your State to this we send back to you; and other[s] who have only took part with Shayes we [go]vern by our laws so that they do not, and dare not make any inroads or devastation in the Massachusetts. –
> As part of the appendix to the Oracles of reason should you procure 18 or 20 pound [sic] by subscription in ready money, it

shall be published next spring. I am sir with respect your Humble Sert.-- Ethan Allen

   Major Royal Tyler

   Boston

   For Major Tyler per favor Majr Hopkins"[8]

Scholar Marius B. Peladeau and others believe the original appendix, which now resides at the Houghton Library at Harvard, was already written by 1787. The library has dated the original manuscript to 1784. But as any author knows, a writer's work is never done, and even finished products are sometimes in revision. Ethan may have worked on other writing projects besides his correspondence while he lived in Burlington, but if he did, they have yet to be found.[9]

Adjusting to Life in Burlington

Fanny delivered Hannibal Montresor Allen at John Collins' Inn in November and presumably moved into the Allen house by the river when she had recovered. On November 12th, Ethan wrote Stephen Rowe Bradley, his attorney in Westminster, about his attempts to retrieve Fanny's one-third share of her stepfather Crean Brush's estate in Westminster. Allen promised to visit Bradley and repay him for buying a portion of the estate at a vendue (tax sale). A few days later, on November 16th, in another letter, Ethan mentioned his recent arrival at his 1,400-acre farm with 350 acres of choice "swaley" rich upland meadow, interspersed with the finest wheatland he ever saw, with 40 acres under improvement. Allen complained that philosophy was not a popular topic in the Burlington area, but "talk is of bullocks and our glory is in the gad." The talk of bullocks was possibly an Old Testament reference to a quote from Ecclesiasticus 38:25. Brother Levi and Ethan, to a lesser extent, were fond of using classical associations and biblical references in their correspondences.[10]

Allen had finally found his forever home—a rustic paradise on a bluff overlooking the beautiful Onion River and its rich intervale soils. By then, his book, *Reason*, was beginning to perturb clergy in the colonies and abroad. An open letter to Ethan Allen Esquire from "Mr. Woolston" in London, published in the May 5th *Vermont Gazette*, accused Allen of plagiarism and warned Allen of the consequences of God's judgment for his blasphemy in the book. Furthermore, the letter charged Allen with hypocrisy and misrepresenting himself with pedantic reason.[11]

There is no evidence that Allen responded directly to this or other personal or philosophical attacks stemming from his book while he was in Burlington. He commented to Stephen Rowe Bradley that he was surprised the reaction to the book from the clergy wasn't worse. The book's appendix, also known as *An Essay on the Universal Plentitude of Being...*, notes on the cover page that it was intended to be published later when it wouldn't "impact my present or future life."[12]

Perhaps Allen was tired of being a lightning rod for his outspoken views. It wasn't as if he was the only one critical of the church in New England. Burlington had no church buildings yet, and it would be ten years after his death before a small group began meeting in Burlington to discuss forming a Congregational Church. But Allen was one of the few who publicly criticized the church and clergy. He knew that the church still had a powerful place in American politics. Allen's philosophy did not go unnoticed by 18th-century Vermont tourists, especially one who left behind a memoir with his pointed sentiments.

When traveling pastor Nathaniel Perkins visited Burlington a couple of years later in 1789, he noted that Vermont was full of heathens and had little religion. The accommodations where Perkins stayed were dark, dirty, and stinky. In defense of early Burlingtonians, the small growing community of yeoman settlers might have had higher priorities than promoting organized religion. There were trees to cut, mill, and sell; cabins to build; land to farm; and mouths to feed.[13]

The collection of surviving documents from Allen's final full year, 1788, is very lean. It could be that he was finally immersed in his life on the farm and was engaged in more local social interactions instead of the business of writing letters. Virtually all his surviving correspondence includes business concerns instead of writing for pleasure.

Perhaps his farm and family had finally taken center stage in his life. And from what little he mentioned in letters to others, he was busy with farm work.

1788-89

As 1787 drew to a close, the Allen family must have been adjusting to their new home and a quieter way of life in Burlington. Business continued on the farm and river, although things slowed down in the winter. On December 19, Levi notified his debtors to remit payments immediately, under the threat of legal suits. Although Levi and Ira submitted a long list of debtors to their attorney, Samuel Hitchcock, there was no indication that Ethan became overextended on credit and had significant debtors or creditors to the extent his brothers did. Ira and Levi both became submerged in debt and never recovered. As we shall see, Ethan's judicious use of IOUs and notes is corroborated by testimonials from his acquaintances and business associates. Financial discipline was uncommon in the days of sparse cash and extensive living on credit.

In mid-January 1788, Levi offered to accompany Henry Cull, a Canadian merchant, to Ira's place at Onion River to meet his two brothers. He mentioned the ice was good on the way to Onion River (i.e., Vermont), and at St. John, he had a ready span of horses and a double sleigh and cariole to make the trip. By then, the ice may have been safe enough for travel on the river.[14]

Low river levels and freezing temperatures eventually stopped the mills during winter. Once spring arrived, the Onion River mills would cut lumber, as Ira had contracted with D. Spear, Stephen Carter, Stephen Davison, Phinehas Bean, and others.

On June 15th, Levi and Ethan met at Ira's Onion River office. They visited Ira's store at the base of Colchester Avenue, along with Ethan's daughters Mary Ann, Lucy Caroline, and Pamela. The three young women with General Allen would have been unusual in the frontier town. Lucy might have caught the eye of the young attorney Samuel

Hitchcock, whom Ira and Levi employed as their attorney. Lucy Caroline enjoyed a courtship and would be married within a year. It was there that Ethan and Levi settled some unfinished business.

Levi paid a debt to Ethan for 100 pounds in cash. In today's money, that would be worth 20,000 pounds, a significant amount when cash of any kind was almost impossible to come by. Perhaps Levi was paying off an outstanding property debt or a secondary note from another debtor.[15]

During the summer, Ethan, Levi, and Ira traveled to Canada to talk with Governor Frederick Haldimand about expanding trade between Vermont and Canada. Ethan wrote a two-page follow-up letter from Quebec to Lord Dorchester (Guy Carleton) about the potential for improving trade and weighing the possibilities of a political allegiance between the U.S. and Great Britain.

On September 18, 1788, Levi attempted to embark on his grand plan voyage to England. Contrary winds delayed Levi's crossing for weeks. He was then somehow delayed for months until February. During those months, he wrote letters to different people as he was preparing to leave for England. His whereabouts noted on each letter, ranged all over Vermont from cousin Ebenezer's Two Heroes Inn in the Lake Champlain islands to southern Vermont and seemingly everywhere but St. John, Quebec, where his wife Nancy ran the store with Prince and little Nancy. It is possible Ethan and Levi met again before Levi departed for London, but we don't know.

In October, Ethan and his friend, Samuel Stearns (1747-1810), wrote a petition to the Vermont Legislature requesting the formation of a moral philosophy society to study and cultivate the science of the same. Stearns was from Massachusetts and had been imprisoned during the war as a Loyalist. After that, he had distinguished himself by publishing *The Northamerican Almanack*, a nautical almanac describing a scientific explanation for the aurora borealis, and practicing as an astronomer and herbalist. He lived in Brattleboro. Perhaps the philosophical society petition gained momentum after conversations with another Allen friend, Hector St. John. St. John would be elected to the American

Philosophical Society in Philadelphia the following year. Allen was impressed enough with Stearns that he proposed to Dartmouth President John Wheelock that Stearns be awarded an honorary degree. Allen had an ongoing dialogue with John Wheelock. In one of those letters, he offered the support of Vermont. They also had deep philosophical discussions. Allen said:

"I have just returned from Quebec... and conversation of Lord Dorchester and Judge Smith, the first civil magestrates of the province &&cc, and to sundry Gentlemen of the army, and other Civil officers, merchants &cc, but they have no very rare intelligence. ... I have held a round of European and American politic's, but all of it amounts merely to theory, and most of it was inspired by good wine and punch, some times the conversation touched lightly on the philosophical Subjects, but you know that most of our Gentlemen, (not including the commander in chief, Judge Smith and two or three more), are above Such dry and insiped conversation;... should they attempt to handle such Subjects, they would disclose their week Side; the drinking and giving of tosts, talking on Subjects of gallantry, and putting on the outside of the gentlemen, better Suits their capacity and inclination, than to Examine into the nature and reason of things. Sir, since our interview at Bennington, I have almost catched an Idea of a mear spirit, or unbodied Soul, but not quite, I apprehen'd you could help me to it, if any man. When we are on the very point of discovering invisible things, they vanish from our imaginations, and leave us gapeing and staring after them, with eyes of flesh like fools. We are told by Enthusiasts and Lunaticks, that they hold a correspondence with mere Spirits, particularly with the Holy Ghost. Weak minds make their silly imaginations pass for reality, though sensible and Learned persons cannot thus impose on themselves, nor be imposed on by others. A competency of knowledge in the Sciences, is therefore our only Bulwark, against Superstition and Idolatry. The Superstitious part of mankind, which by one means or other, are far the most numerous, are but the dupes of Church and State, at their command they cut one anothers throats, as they suppose for Gods Sake, and commit all manner of cruelty and outrage..."[16]

Wheelock responded:

"Printers inherit the spirit of their Sires for they aim more to alarm and please mankind, than to inform their understanding. The liberty of the press has been idolized to extravigancy for that which ought to be the arsenal of truth has become the forge of falsehood. Mankind somehow or other are pleased with Fanciful errors more than with truth; the Philosopher alone dispises fiction; he is even raised above the probable, and dwells in the realms of truths. To reason Systimatically is to pass up from effects to thier causes. The capacity of the mind is limited, its view consequently circumscribed; and should it estimate the cause by only what it can clearly comprehend in the effects, it might at once reject the idea of an omnipotent Creator; but there are many facts the circumstances and cause whose existence the mind cannot encircle. The harmonious creation and design of these waft the reflection to unbounded intellegence and power. The observations in your letters give me much pleasure; and from my idea of your philsophic and contemplative turn, persuaded I am that you will by sublime reason pervade the maze of atheism into the region of theism."[17]

President Wheelock would never see Allen use sublime reason to "pervade the maze of atheism into the region of theism." Wheelock's final letter, written February 13, 1789, would never reach Allen's hand. No other correspondences survive from Allen's final year, his first and only full year in Burlington. The traces of the past only hint at the happenings and complex lives intertwined at the homestead during that time.

Although the farm thrived in some respects, 1788 was another unproductive crop year. But the weather wasn't the only factor. Allen's acreage had been in production for as many as 15 years since Felix Powell bought it in the early 1770s. The fertile topsoil was depleted of nutrients by the mid-1780s. Barren soil due to farming practices that lacked fertilizer and mechanical farming tools would have only added to farmers' low crop yields.

14

Ethan and Fanny's Home
1787 - 1789

The existing 1780s "Ethan Allen house" on the Ethan Allen Homestead Park site matches the dimensions of the house Ethan asked Ira to build him. The building includes posts, beams, some 18th-century-era hand-made nails, and dimensional lumber. Some of the beams and boards show reciprocating saw marks on the surface of the wood. Reciprocating (back-and-forth) saws were in use during the 18th century and would have matched the original saws in Ira Allen's mill several miles up the river.

Many historians believe it is plausible that the house was the Allens' home between 1787 and 1790 and the Penniman family's home during the 1790s. Generations of farmers continued to use it as a farmhouse, and it was renovated many times for 200 years after the Allens left.

Ethan brought six cows to the

The Allen House at the Ethan Allen Homestead Museum.
EAHM

farm. Besides a yoke of oxen, according to a statement by Fanny to her lawyer Udney Hay, the Allen farm likely included several beef cattle on the hoof, a bull, calves, mares, sheep, pigs, hogs, a horse, and one or more colts. The Allens had ample time in the fall to preserve as much food as possible and get it into cold storage in the crawl space under the house. They preserved beef and hogs from the fall slaughter using salt.[1]

Subsequent owners added several more outbuildings over the years, which all eventually burned. It is unknown whether Ira built another house for Ethan, on the intervale or elsewhere, as he had promised to do in their 1787 ORLC termination agreement.[2]

Ethan, Fanny, the four young Allen women, baby Hannibal, and possibly three or more servants would have likely shared the 1600-square-foot house. It might have been the birthplace of Ethan Alphonso Allen in October of 1789. A family of 10 or more people inhabiting a home of that size was not unusual during the 18th century, but by today's standards, they were crowded. Settlers rarely designated rooms as bedrooms, and their personal space was minimal. Barns and other outbuildings offered workspace and added value to the cozy living spaces. People attended to nature's private needs using outhouses sited away from the house.

The original foundation of the Allen house building consisted of dolomite limestone quarry rock, which also comprised the original hearths, fireplaces, and central chimney. The rock was likely sourced on the property, possibly from 100 yards away, out of ledge rocks near the marsh on the southeast side of the house.

Generations of renovations altered the original house, with dozens of tenants coming and going and many owners over 238 years. The original foundation had only a crawlspace, which was standard then, not a full basement that exists today. Some of the post and beam hand-hewn timbers with mortise and tenon joints and planks survived the 19th and 20th-century construction that added dormers in the roof and an attached ell that was added on the west side of the building. In the 1980s, the ell wing of the house was removed and rolled across the yard to become the white clapboard caretaker's house, which sits today next to the Brownell Education Center.[3]

During the 1980s historic renovation, the original main structure was jacked up and gutted to evaluate and reconstruct with historical accuracy. Contractors replaced all of the original windows and most of the first story floorboards using 18th-century materials from similar homes. The brick fireplaces that exist now were built during the 19th or 20th century renovations after the Allens left. Other work has taken place to mitigate drainage and humidity problems in the cellar and to slow the rotting of beams and planks.[4]

Allen and others constructed outbuildings on the property. In the 1790s, Jabez Penniman built a large carriage barn. Photos from the early 20th century show several barns near the house, and prior research shows the original barns sat on the east and south sides of the house. There are burn marks from a barn fire on some of the east elevation attic timbers. When historian Ralph Nading Hill discovered the house in the 1980s, there were no windows on the south side of the house, and no nearby outbuildings were left.[5]

The high ground the home sits on was surrounded by a flood plain traditionally planted with corn and wheat. Being near the water was advantageous for commerce, transportation, and fishing. The original soils were rich in nutrients from old growth forests and the floodplain. Still, there was no irrigation or ability to move water up to the higher elevation fields until long after the Allens left.[6]

The river was a main thoroughfare and flowed with shipping and personal and commercial watercraft. The Allens would have had some watercraft on the river. It was easy to row, paddle, skate, or walk to Ira's place up the river a couple of miles east toward the falls and mills. To get to Burlington Bay, which was becoming the town center, a trail led south, or they could take a longer route down the river into the lake and paddle five miles around Sunset Cliff and Appletree Point into the bay.

Only a few cleared paths connected the bay and the river in 1787. Water Street and today's Pearl Street ran from the bay to the falls. A simple north-south and east-west grid of paths sketched by Levi Allen's brother-in-law William Coit mapped a grid that defined the original downtown. Swine and cows roamed the paths as the town steadily morphed from forest into farms. Bears foraged on the top of the hill where UVM is today.

In letters to his merchant brother Levi, Ethan complained about his wheat crop production due to a backward spring, which began with a warm start, a cold spring-summer season, and unstable rainfall during the 1788 growing season. Allen grew wheat, corn, peas, squash, pumpkins, flax for linen, medicinal plants, dyes, and other food crops on the farm. He raised and sold beef, which needed grain and water as well. Oxen hauled silty water up from the river for the animals.

The Burlington growing season microclimate may have been longer than in Sunderland since the Lake Champlain Valley stayed relatively warmer into the fall. But being 100 miles north of Sunderland meant it was generally a few degrees colder. And it felt frigid once the lake and river froze and the winter wind chills took over.

An uninsulated home like the Allen house would have been chilly, even with an unlimited firewood supply. A starter home log cabin would have been better insulated, more efficient, and more comfortable, but the fact that Allen wanted a frame house tells us he was accustomed to a middle-class lifestyle. The Allens likely burned 10 to 20 cords of wood a year in their fireplaces, and it still would have been drafty in the corners and near the frosted-over single-pane windows. Based on the modern surveys of the building, inhabitants had never directly heated the upstairs of the house. The two upper-floor rooms felt bitter cold most of the winter and often mercilessly hot in the summer, especially without windscreen evergreens or shade trees nearby. The crawl space was a perfect root cellar and storage cellar for sugar or salt brine preserves, salted and smoked meat, and kegs of rum and cider.[7]

It was customary for families to eat together, with adults and older kids sitting at the table. Usually, they shared a mug of beverage around the table. Hence, biographers have often used the term "flowing bowls." A husband and wife would frequently share a plate of food between them, although we don't know if this was the case with Ethan and Fanny. The servants would eat with the family, customarily standing and eating during dinner. After dinner, it was not uncommon to sit around a warm fire before retiring early to a straw mattress or bed off the cold floor, if lucky. The Allen's employees stayed with the family, and people would have been sleeping throughout the building, not necessarily confining sleep quarters to one or two designated bedrooms.[8]

One unintended consequence of sharing containers and living in tight quarters was the ease of passing infectious diseases. Smallpox and tuberculosis were common during an era that preceded knowledge about microbes. Only two of Mary Brownson's children reached adulthood, and Mary died at 51. Ethan and Fanny's children somehow fared better. Disease prevention was unheard of, and treatments were byzantine compared to our best practices of medicine today. Bloodletting was a common cure-all. Commonplace medicines included substances such as mercury calomel, lead apatite, alcoholic drinks, and laudanum, an alcohol tincture of opium are now known to be toxic. Today, in hindsight, we can appreciate how the Hippocratic oath of "do no harm" has improved medical practice over the centuries. There were no doctors known to have lived in Burlington before 1790.

Several acquaintances, including his brother Ira, noted that Allen's years in captivity with a poor diet, immobility, and torture devastated his health. In his autobiography, Ira noted Ethan's diminished state as a result of his imprisonment. Not to mention a lifetime of heavy drinking, ubiquitous tobacco smoking, and possibly genetic factors that were catching up with him by the time he arrived in Burlington. According to Huldah Lawrence, one of Allen's family friends, Allen had suffered a couple of "fits," i.e., strokes, during their time in Burlington. He knew he had some potentially serious health problems and expected to eventually "die in a fit." Vermont's long, cold seasons didn't help.[9,10]

The northern winter season extended from November through the maple sap run in March. Slowly, the ice on the river and lake melted and was out by April, and the glorious spring sun arrived to awaken nature's plants and animals. The runoff from the melting, swollen streams, and rivers powered the mills again. Along with the warming soil and spring rains came the farming rituals of clearing, plowing, planting, fencing, caring for animals, and the never-ending job of harvesting timber and cutting and splitting firewood. Most of this work continued through the summer. Farmers had not learned about soil amendments, conservation practices, and mechanization until the 1800s.

By 1789, even though Allen still had unfulfilled dreams and work to do, the Allen family life was about to change drastically. One of the Allen farm hands was 17-year-old Hawley Witters (1772-1862). Witters later described in a letter that Allen was honest and "very kind" to Fanny, whom he described as a "clever" woman. Witters described Ethan: "He always paid his men well, but they had to stir about and tend to their business. Used to drink hard at times. Was a pretty tall man— pretty red faced."[11]

Ethan, Fanny, and Ira were intimate friends with Burlington Constable Stephen Lawrence and his wife, Mary. Their daughter, Huldah Lawrence, who was six years old in 1789, would later recall that Ethan would take the family down the frozen river during winter to Colchester Point or Burlington Bay on an ox sled. This trip would have been a time-consuming adventure at today's almost inconceivably slow pace of two miles per hour.[12]

The Family of Ethan Allen and
Fanny Montresor Brush Buchanan Allen:

Ethan Allen married (1784) Fanny Montresor Brush Buchanan
(1760-1834)
Frances (Fanny) Margaret Allen (1784-1819)
Hannibal Montresor Allen (1787-1813) married (1808) Agnes
Bodine (1788-1763)
Ethan Alphonso Allen (1789-1855) married (1817) Mary Susana
Johnson (1797-1818)
- married (1820) Martha Washington Johnson (1802-1855)[13]

III

Family Ties Under Strain

15

Ethan Allen's Unexpected Death February 12, 1789

The story of Ethan Allen's death and funeral has been told and retold throughout the past couple of hundred years with different proportions of accuracy and mythology. This account is derived directly from primary sources and the most objective records. From Allen's letters, we know the summer of 1788 was a terrible growing season in Burlington. By midwinter of 1788-1789, Ethan had plenty of beef but needed hay for his livestock.

The republic of Vermont had deeded the Green Mountain Boys lots in the Two Heroes, now known as the islands of North Hero and Grand Isle, which includes the town of South Hero. At least a handful of Boys lived on the island or nearby North Hero. War hero Colonel Ebenezer Allen had picked a 64-acre lot on the southern tip of South Hero. The year the Allens moved to Burlington, Ebenezer added a wood frame tavern called the Two Heroes Inn, a popular establishment on the island. The island soil and microclimate had yielded a surplus of hay that year.

Vermont Ox sled
Library of Congress

On Tuesday, February 10, Ethan headed northwest over the iced-over Onion River and up the frozen lake on his ox sled with Newport, his farmhand. At a plodding trot of two miles per hour, the trip would take at least five or six hours over the ice, without a headwind, if the oxen were motivated. Ethan planned to get a load of hay, stay overnight, get up early the next day, and head back to the homestead in Burlington.

Although remarkable legends persist about Ebenezer summoning a great multitude of Green Mountain Boys who drank endless "flowing bowls" of punch, stonewalls, and flips and told stories all night, there are scant primary source accounts of the evening's activities with the aging Boys. If Ethan had made prior plans, they would have been weather-dependent and could vary either way by a day or two. It would have been easy for Ebenezer to spread the word to a few folks door-to-door that General Allen was stopping by to get hay. But communication at that time was slow. Some biographers may have exaggerated the size of the crowd. According to a witness who spoke to Ethan's driver, Ethan arose before dawn on Wednesday, hopped on a sled piled with hay, and headed back across the ice at the ox team's pace, one step at a time, for the five or six-hour trip to Burlington.

Anyone who lives near the lake in the Champlain Valley knows the wind blows regularly. A steady 10-15 mile per hour wind that blows for days on end is ordinary. Winds reach over 30 miles per hour or more every month. We don't know if there was a wind. Still, we know the long-term historic average nighttime low temperature for February 11 is eight degrees Fahrenheit and considered dangerously cold. This temperature creates an exposure risk in just a few minutes, let alone being exposed for hours. Even light winds could have pushed the wind chill below zero.[1]

Two accounts published in the *Burlington Free Press* describe what happened next. On June 18, 1858, two Burlington residents, Huldah Lawrence and Henry Collins, both gave sworn testimonies of their memories of the Allen family years in Burlington before Justice of the Peace Isaiah Huntley. According to folklore, when the sled approached the mouth of the river, some biographers report that Ethan commented to his farmhand Newport, "It seems as though the trees are very thick here," but the source doesn't show that quote.

Henry Collins described Newport's account of the trip to the homestead. The sled approached the mouth of the river, still two and a half miles from the homestead. Allen erupted in a violent fit, and he struggled for 30 to 45 minutes and had to be restrained by Newport to keep him from falling off the haystack. Then Allen slumped over and lost consciousness. After traveling the final hours up the river ice, they arrived at the homestead in the afternoon. Newport carried the unconscious Allen into the house and laid him in bed. A confused Fanny quickly moved into the other room.[2]

According to some biographers, but not definitively cited in primary sources, one of Ethan's acquaintances, a Burlington tooth-puller named Steven Law, who was not a medical doctor, attempted bloodletting, a common remedy for many ailments at the time. If this occurred, it further damaged Allen's chances of recovery and survival. Nonetheless,

Allen never regained consciousness and passed away at 9:00 AM the following day, February 12, according to Hawley Witters, an employee.[3]

Fanny sent a man to call Stephen and Mary Lawrence to Allen's bedside, but by the time they arrived, Ethan was dead. Their six-year-old daughter Huldah Lawrence saw the deceased Allen on his bed at the house. Fanny made arrangements for his burial to take place a few days later. When the Lawrences and others arrived on the burial day, Ira had moved Ethan's body to his home across the river. Ira had returned from a trip to Manchester and claimed Ethan had expressed his wish to be buried with military honors.[4]

Ira later wrote that Ethan died of "arperplexy." Apoplexy was the term used to describe an ischemic stroke. This kind of stroke results when the blood supply to the brain is restricted, which prevents oxygen and nutrients from getting to brain cells. Nowadays, we know that the risk of ischemic stroke significantly increases during cold weather. Even without any alcohol consumption that may or may not have occurred at Two Heroes Inn, the possible early morning frigid air could have been enough to trigger Allen's stroke, based on current research.[5,6]

Ira took a few days to arrange a proper internment and took the body up and across the river to Colchester. Ethan's body lay in a coffin facing the river at Ira's house. He sent out word of the funeral at noon on February 16. Only one person had been buried in the burying yard at the top of the rolling hill in Burlington, and Ethan would become the second.[7]

16

The Aftermath - February 1789

On a cold, sunny February 16, after a dusting of snow, a throng of mourners gathered at Ira's home. According to John Knicke-bacor's memoir, Ira had a 1 1/2-story Georgian house with a hip roof. It sat on the present location of the Winooski block on the corner of East Allen and Main Street.

Ira tapped a keg of rum. Ethan's friend, Major Bill Goodrich of Vergennes, marshaled the procession of mourners with a military honor guard with a cannon in tow. The crowd marched to muffled drum beats across the river ice and up the hill to the "burying yard" in Burlington, called Greenmount Cemetery today.[1]

The procession paused for a cannon salute every minute. Militiamen placed the coffin over the grave and placed two swords on it. They removed the swords and opened the coffin for a few minutes, then closed it for the last time. Once they lowered the coffin into the grave, six platoons fired several volleys of muskets. [2,3]

The *Vermont Gazette* reprinted the following account on March 16, 1789:

"Last Thursday, departed this life, by a fit of the apoplexy, the Hon. Maj. General ETHAN ALLEN, in the 54th year of his age; yesterday his remains were recently interred. The following was the order of the procession to his grave:

1. The artillery firing minute guns.
2. A company of infantry with trail'd arms.
3. Six field officers with drawn swords.
4. The CORPSE, his excellency The GOVERNOR. A Maj. Gen. and four field officers.
5. The MOURNERS.
6. Officers of different ranks by two and two.
7. Civil Magistrates.
8. Spectators.

"When the remains were laid in the grave, three volleys of musquetry were discharged by the infantry; after which three cannons. The remains being interred, the troops &c. Returned from the grave in proper order. The whole was attended with the greatest decorum. And everyone present to manifest a wish to render his burial honourable as his character had ever been respectable."[4]

Family friend Henry Collins remembered that Major Goodrich made a few remarks to the people, referring to what Mr. Allen had done for the country and how he had suffered for it. That account, along with Allen's death certificate, pins the date of Allen's death as Thursday, February 12th. They placed a wooden plank with his name over Allen's Grave.[5,6]

In 1789, the cemetery was still in its forest state. It included tree stumps and had yet to be cleared. Somewhere along the way in the years after his burial, Allen's wood gravemarker disappeared. Jabez Penniman bought and installed a marble marker in 1808.

As more Revolutionary War-era settlers died off and Vermonters continued to build their lives and tackle tough economic times, the

War of 1812 flared up with a huge battle in the Champlain Valley. With the march of time, the personal and institutional memories of the 18th-century Green Mountain Boys waned. The presence of Allen and other founders drifted away from consciousness as did the seeming permanence they once had. In the 1850s, long after Jabez Penniman was gone, questions arose about the exact location of Allen's remains when it came time to commemorate the site with a monument over his grave.[7]

The questions about his grave created mystery, speculation, resulting in years of conspiracy theories and even absurd rumors about what had transpired with Ethan Allen's remains. The speculation was far-ranging and even amusing to nonfiction historians and doesn't deserve repeating.

On June 14, 1858, Ira Allen's son, Ira Hayden Allen, wrote a letter to John Norton Pomeroy, who, along with George Perkins Marsh, was in charge of the Ethan Allen Monument Committee tasked with installing a monument. Ira Hayden Allen's letter should have ended the questions. In the letter, Ira Hayden Allen explained that they had found General Allen's remains in the very spot where those who had attended the funeral said he was buried. Those in attendance included his uncle, Judge Heman "Chili" Allen. Ethan's remains were under the marble tablet erected by Jabez Penniman. The letter said this should end the rumors and that the sparring in the papers about Allen's remains is "mere trash." Shortly after that, word spread far and wide that Ethan's remains were, in fact, intact.[8]

The *Burlington Free Press* reported that while excavating and preparing for the monument, they found remnants of the coffin, Allen's skull, skeleton, and hand directly beneath the marble tombstone. Judge Udney Hay Penniman, the son of Fanny and Jabez Penniman, elaborated that the new excavations dug two feet deeper than previous attempts. The deep burial might explain why previous searches turned up empty-handed.[9]

This news sparked interest outside of Burlington. Larkin Mead, the famous sculptor who eventually created the Ethan Allen statues in Montpelier and the Capitol in Washington, DC, wrote to George Perkins Marsh and Pomeroy. Mr. Mead noted that he had read about the discovery of Allen's remains beneath his old tombstone in his local paper. Mead asked if he could examine the remains and "secure a cast of the skull" to help him create his model for the cemetery statue. He was ready to "come up and make the casts."

Ethan Allen's Greenmount Cemetery grave monument in Burlington.
Author photo.

There is no evidence that Allen's exhumation led to anything other than a deep, prompt, and proper reburial. Due to a lack of available funding, the Ethan Allen statue project stalled for another 15 years and was not completed until 1873 by a different sculptor, Peter Stephenson of Boston. Eventually, they installed the 40-foot-tall marble column and statue that we see today on the site of Allen's grave.[10]

Even though there were puzzles, inconsistencies, and questions surrounding Ethan's life and death, his friends and acquaintances remembered one particular trait: his character. From the *Vermont Journal*:

"It is with much regret that we announce to the public the death of General ETHAN ALLEN, who expired in an epileptic fit on Tuesday last; the patriotism and strong attachment which he ever appeared uniform in the breast of this Great Man, was worthy his exalted character: the public have to lament the loss of a man who has rendered them great service, both in council and in arms; and his family an indulgent friend and tender parent: he has left a most amiable young widow and three small children- and three amiable young daughters of his first wife. While they are deluged in tears for the loss of their best friend, they have the consolation of being left with a handsome fortune."[11]

Accolades of Allen's strong character echoed from colleagues and associates following his passing. Silas "Baron" Hathaway, a Vermont attorney and land speculator and a primary antagonist and creditor of Ira Allen, had this to say about Ethan: "Though possessing many eccentricities, peculiar to himself, [Ethan] exhibited, through his life, a strong sense of honor, and an invincible spirit of patriotism." Hathaway noted that Allen didn't give bonds or IOUs and even left cash to pay three men his unpaid bills.[12]

Some men didn't like Ethan, including high-profile acquaintances Colonel Seth Warner, General Jacob Bayley, and others, not to mention those who accused him of treason for negotiating with British General Governor Haldimand during the early 1780s. Reverend Nathan Perkins would visit his grave "in pious horror." The 'hero of Ticonderoga" and "clodhopper philosopher" was a highly-visible, complex man who attracted attention from admirers and enemies due to his strong political and religious convictions and actions, if nothing else. His iconic name would live on in the folklore and descendants of his family for generations.

The Family Regroups

Unfortunately for his heirs, the ensuing paper trail following Allen's death shows no immediate "handsome fortune" awaiting them, as was predicted in his obituary. It would eventually take years of lawsuits by three different factions of the Allen family to win back Ethan's property from debtors, squatters, fraudulent deeds, or overdue settlements from Ira related to the ORLC.

Court records show that Fanny and Jabez Penniman, Lucy and

Samuel Hitchcock, and other plaintiffs won judgments against Ira Allen, Jonathan Ormsby, Thaddeus Tuttle, and others. In the immediate term, Fanny faced some difficult times. She was a single mother without the rights and power that women have today, and she would soon learn she was pregnant.[13,14]

On October 24, 1789, Fanny delivered Ethan Alphonso Allen, their third child, in Burlington. Oddly, historians John Spargo and John Barr maintain that "Ethan Voltaire" was born in 1786 in Sunderland. Spargo goes as far as to say his name was "Ethan Voltaire," and General Ethan Allen wrote the name "Ethan Voltaire" in his copy of *Reason*. Spargo's story claims that when Fanny married Jabez Penniman, they changed the boy's middle name to Allen; hence, he became "Ethan Allen Allen." No other primary references to middle names Voltaire or Allen can be found. This account from a reputable historian exemplifies how history can be misinterpreted, repeated, and reinforced over time. His gravestone marker in Elmwood Cemetery says Ethan Alphonso Allen 1789-1855. His West Point graduation notice lists him as Ethan A. Allen, aged 66 years, with his death year in 1855. This indicates his birth year was 1789.[15,16,17]

Sarah Owen Allen, brother Heber's widow, who was working and living at Ira's home, had died in 1787. Some historians think Sarah's death prompted Ira to marry Jerusha Enos in 1790, and she became Ira's business partner. This might have changed the Ira Allen family dynamics.[18,19]

At the time of Ethan's death, Lucy Caroline was engaged to the most eligible bachelor around, a Harvard Phi Beta Kappa fraternity man named Samuel Hitchcock. They married two months later, in April. According to Vermont historian David Bryan, Lucy Caroline's two full sisters, Mary Ann and Pamela, went to live with the newlyweds.

Some historians speculate about an alleged rift between Lucy Caroline, Pamela, and Mary Ann, the older Allen siblings, and Fanny. The rift is plausible for several possible reasons that resulted in a personality conflict. Fanny might have presented as a starkly different, younger mother figure than Mary Brownson. Fanny had come from a completely different social class and culture that the sisters may have eschewed while growing up in modest circumstances in an arduous farm life. They were closer to Fanny's age than their father, Ethan. They were also in their teen and young adult years, with their own lives and dreams, and maybe felt upstaged by the younger Fanny Margaret, Hannibal, and Ethan Alphonso. Perhaps Lucy Caroline, Mary Ann, and Pamela still carried unresolved grief or felt an allegiance to the memory of their deceased mother. There is evidence of a family rift.

All accounts say Fanny stayed in Burlington for about a year after Ethan's death, and records show she paid some debts to laborers. Fanny's friend Mary Lawrence was also a grieving widow after losing her husband Stephen in April, and the two may have been supportive of each other.[20]

By 1790, Fanny returned to Westminster with little Fanny and infants Hannibal and Ethan to live with Margaret and Patrick Wall. Ira found tenants who would rent the farm and keep it in production. Ira was the administrator of Ethan's intestate estate, but he stalled probate for years, perhaps because he knew the real estate assets would appreciate in time as the economy improved. Even though the ORLC was dissolved, Ira had not lived up to the terms of their agreement with money, acreage, or store credit. Although this agreement appeared to settle Ethan's partnership with the ORLC, Ethan died leaving his heirs without benefitting much from the contract. Consequently, Ethan's heirs were counting on Ira to settle the estate.

The relationship between Fanny and her stepdaughter Lucy and her husband Samuel Hitchcock, at least below the surface, was strained and disingenuous. A surviving letter illustrates this. In 1791, Samuel Hitchcock wrote a letter to Lucy, complaining about Lucy's step-mother, Fanny:

"I shall be obliged to call & See our chaste, discreet & *virtuous* mother—shall I express a great deal of love to her on your account? — I shall be glad to see the little boys and on this account shall call—but I should be happily disappointed if she should be from home."[21]

We wonder if Fanny knew about their disparaging comments or if she would have cared. Fanny employed attorney Udney Hay to assist her in transitioning to her new reality. With the help of Ethan's friend and attorney Stephen Rowe Bradley in Westminster and others, Fanny, Margaret, and Patrick Wall had managed to reclaim the legal title to the former Crean Brush house as their home, which was the most valuable piece of Brush's 60,000 acres in Vermont they were able to retrieve. The British government partially reimbursed the Walls as Loyalists, and Patrick continued his business as a tailor. In 1791, the U.S. Congress finally admitted Vermont to the union. Stephen Bradley, one of the architects of Vermont statehood, had been elected as one of Vermont's first two U. S. Senators.

Fanny reacquainted herself with families she had known in New York that had since moved to Vermont or nearby New Hampshire, but Ethan's inheritance and her marriage bond were still not forthcoming. Within a few years, Fanny's life would encounter another significant change.[22]

17

The Pennimans 1793

In October 1793, Fanny married Dr. Jabez Penniman, whom she had met in Westminster. Dr. Penniman was four years younger than Fanny, a physician, an astute businessman, and a high-achiever. They were married at a friend's house and moved into Penniman's home. In the spring of 1794, they moved back into the Ethan Allen Homestead without Ira's permission as the executor of Ethan's estate. Although Fanny hadn't received any inheritance from Ethan's estate and the coverture laws were unfavorable to widows, the court might have defended her right to the property since she had settled there with Ethan and their family. Dr. Penniman's practice supported the young Penniman family in the small town of Burlington, which still had a population of under 1,000 up until 1800.[1,2]

During the next few years, Fanny gave birth to three more children. Her literacy showed with her choice of names for the Penniman children: Hortensia Monemia, which is a garden reference; Udney Hay, the namesake of the Pennimans' Deist friend and attorney; and Julietta Octavia, possibly named after Julius and Octavian Ceasar of Rome. Their youngest, Adelia, meaning "noble," was born in 1800 after the Pennimans left Burlington for a few years to live in Swanton while

Jabez served as collector of customs. After that experience, they finally settled on a large farm in Colchester.

When Adelia was 15, she and her mother, Fanny, collected and cataloged their wildflower collection, documenting common names, scientific names, and floriography. Floriography, popular at that time, imparted messages for different flowers. For example, roses show a crush, forget-me-nots a farewell, and petunias resentment. Fanny and Adelia's colorful collection still survives today with their handwritten labels at the UVM Pringle Herbarium.

Margaret Brush raised Fanny to study the Greek and Roman classics, botany, Latin language, and cultures. Margaret gave her access to the best authors, including French botanists Andre and Francois Michaux, who had visited Burlington on separate occasions around the turn of the century. Francois published a book on horticulture and scientific vocabulary in the early 1800s. This book would have given Fanny knowledge of cutting-edge botany and taxonomy and might have inspired her flower collection.[3,4]

Despite Fanny's talents, the Allen family members' loyalty to Fanny varied. Ethan and Levi weren't close, but Levi had mentioned he was glad to see Fanny support Ethan and "make everything easy" on him. But a rift had developed between Fanny and Ira. In February of 1802, Fanny's husband, Jabez Penniman, had written to Ira on her behalf to persuade Ira to pay for Hannibal's and Ethan's educations. As Penniman said:

"But—Sir—It was Mrs. Penniman's particular desire to know on what conditions I left them—I conceive for myself that you take the charge on yourself and be at the expense of their Board Clothing and Education in future and exonerate me—as I have been at great expense for ten years past—You will be so good as to write me plain and explicit on the subject that I can be able to show Mrs. Penniman how I have disposed of her *Orphan Children* and ease the feelings of an ancious Mother"[5]

Ira sent John Allen Finch, Heman "Chili" Allen, and other nephews to college. Paying for the education of his nephews Hannibal and Ethan

Alphonso would not have been out of character. Unfortunately, Ira had just been released from years in French and British incarceration, and he had a world of problems, not the least of which was widespread intractable debt. Levi had just died in pauper's prison. If British and French confinement hadn't dampened his spirits, returning to face a crowd of creditors was the turning point of Ira's tumultuous fall from grace. He was looking to trim expenditures in any way he could. After Ethan died, Ira took responsibility for the education of Hannibal and Ethan Alphonso. What happened when he discovered that Dr. Penniman had become their guardian? On June 12, 1802, an irate Ira Allen wrote to Fanny from Colchester:

> "Doctr Penniman Brought your sons to me & Left them in my Care. I immeeately put Hanible into Collage & Ethan in School with my sons where they are doing as well as might be Expected—But to my supprise after Mr. Penniman was gone I was Informed that he had found means to Get himself appointed thier guardian. I Enquired of Hanible how he Came to appoint Mr. Penniman his Guardian. He s'd Mr. P. informed him that he had Consulted me & that I had agreed to it. I Positively Declare that I had not the most Distant Idea of such appointment and assure you that However dear the sons of a Respected & Deceast Brother may be to me I will not have anything to do with thier Education Under the Guardeanship of any Man in Existance. Therefore my Letter to Doctr Penniman of this Date must be Complyed with & I Receive Returns by Mrs. [Jerusha, Ira's wife] Allen who is on a Visset to see a Number of her frends on Connecticut River or their Guardean must Immediately take Charge of them. Be assured that this Letter is the Result of mature Deliberation and that at all Times I shall feel it a Duty I owe to the Memory of my Borther & you as Parent to three of his Children to advise with you for their best Good as occasions may from Time to time Require—Mrs. Allen will more fully Explain my Reasons for Writing you this Letter and inform you of

some other things that may be usefull to you in more ways than one & which I have not time to State in a Letter—Give my Best Compliments to Mr. Wall Mrs. Wall & Miss Fanny."[6]

Ethan's widow and the boys weren't the only ones irking Ira. By 1801, Ira's former friend, Silas "Baron" Hathaway, an attorney and land speculator, sued Ira Allen. As noted earlier, after 1804, Ira disappeared from most Vermonters' minds while living out his final decade in Philadelphia. However, his creditors still sought to bring him to justice and settle their accounts against him. Ira's wife Jerusha and their kids stayed in the Colchester area. Heber's son, attorney Heman Allen, successfully maneuvered and protected Jerusha's Irasburg land from creditors.[7]

Jabez and Fanny Penniman eventually moved to a farm on the east side of Lime Kiln Road in Colchester, across from present-day Saint Michael's College on Route 15. Their farmhouse had beautiful southern hillside views of the Green Mountain range and plenty of sunny exposure. It was near the river and the main road to Essex Junction and Jericho. Jabez was caring for the ailing mother of attorney Stephen Rowe Bradley, and several letters to Bradley updated him on her condition and infirmities.

The Pennimans and Bradleys were close personal friends, and their correspondence was conciliatory. Jabez passed on Fanny's well-wishes and pleasantries to others, including the Bradleys, but handwritten correspondence that Fanny might have penned throughout her life didn't survive. In one letter from March 1804, Penniman mentioned that Fanny was giving her only copy of *Reason* to Bradley. In another letter, Penniman expressed Fanny's compliments, saying, "Mrs Penniman and Miss Fanny Allen join me in respects to yourself and Mrs. Bradley — Fanny proposes to visit Westminster in May, when she will pay her personal respects to yourself and her much esteemed friend, your good Lady."[8]

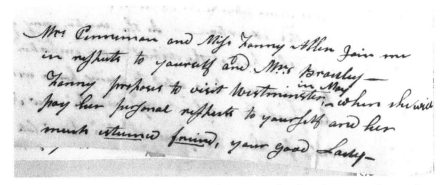

Jabez Penniman's note expressing Fanny's desire to "pay her formal respects to her much esteemed friend, your good Lady."
UVMSC, author photo.

By 1808, both Hannibal Montresor Allen (Class of 1806) and Ethan Alphonso Allen had graduated from West Point. Ethan Alphonso was 19, and on March 1st, he wrote a letter from Fort Constitution, New Hampshire, to his cousin, Ira's son Zimry Enos Allen. It appears that Ethan's mother, Fanny, and stepfather, Jabez Penniman, raised objections to his matrimonial ambitions and convinced him to cool his impulses until he was more financially able.

In the letter, Ethan talked about recently being in Colchester and elaborated on his ascension into the officer's ranks and future career opportunities in the army. He also had something to say to his cousin about his parents' interjecting their opinions into his personal life.

Ethan Alphonso wrote:

> "I am head over ears in love with a fine young Lady, but dare not proceed further on account of the Displeasure of my Parents and which is full and great an obstacle to the union is my use and circumstances in life; when I make myself Master of the Mines of Peru, I shall then get me a companion."[9]

A month later, during the heat of President Thomas Jefferson's unpopular embargo prohibiting trade with Canada, an open letter to the president was printed in the *Burlington Sentinel and Democrat* signed "Ethan Allen." During that time, letters signed with pen names were not unusual. Fact-checking op-ed writer identities wasn't what it is today. It is possible the letter came from someone other than Ethan.

Remember, Jabez Penniman had accepted President Jefferson's appointment as U.S. Collector of Customs, putting him in the difficult position of trying to stop rampant armed smuggling at a time when Vermonters were utterly dependent on trade with Canada. The same April 15th newspaper edition included letters from Penniman supporting the embargo and "Allen" condemning the embargo. The embargo conflict had reached a fever pitch in Vermont, but neither writer could foresee the mortal bloodshed during the Black Snake Affair coming in a few months.

In Penniman's words: "Rafts as well as vessels must be prevented from proceeding to a Foreign Port, and for that purpose, one or two armed boats may, if necessary, be stationed near to the line, at the lower end of your district."

In the same edition of the paper, the opposing letter, humbly submitted to the president, began: "This fag end of the Embargo goes to prohibit the farmers of Vermont and New Hampshire from driving their swine into Canada for sale..." The letter ended with the sentiment that the embargo was an "anti-republican act." If Ethan Alphonso indeed wrote this letter, it would make for some exciting dinner conversations during the Allen-Penniman family get-togethers.[10]

Penniman must have known that smugglers were arming their crews with guns, creating a dangerous situation for the federal militiamen he hired to enforce the embargo. In August, on the Winooski River, not far from the Ethan Allen Homestead, several men were killed by smugglers on the Black Snake, a lake ferry converted for smuggling. A murder trial ensued, Cyrus Dean was convicted of murder and subsequently executed by hanging in Burlington. According to William Rann in *The History of Chittenden County*, they built a scaffold on the east side of Prospect Street, east of Mary Fletcher's house. The executioner hung Cyrus Dean in front of a large crowd.[11]

The Family of Jabez Penniman and
Fanny Montresor Brush Buchanan Allen Penniman:

Jabez Penniman (1764-1841) married (1793) Fanny Montresor Brush
Buchanan Allen(1760-1834)

Hortensia Monemia Penniman (1795-1827) married William
Brayton (1812)

Udney Hay Penniman (1796-1862) married Maria Boynton (d. 1834)

Julietta Octavia Penniman (1793-1883) married Nathan Ryno Smith
(1797-1877)

Adelia Agusta Penniman (1801-1884) married Dr. Robert Moody
(1801-1841)[12, 13]

18

The Next Generations
1789-1870

Fanny and Ethan's first child, Fanny Margaret, was born in November 1784 in Sunderland, and her life was a long, celebrated story. She was only five when her father died in Burlington. After his death, she lived with her widowed mother and her siblings for a year, then with the Walls in Westminster for a few years. During that time, one story is Fanny Margaret was attacked by a serpent while playing by herself near the river. A mysterious robed man appeared and warned her she shouldn't play there. Fanny promptly ran back to her house. Years later, in a French school in Montreal, she recognized the robed man who had approached her as a saint in a painting at the Roman Catholic church where she worked. This religious experience led to her becoming a nun. Many biographers consider this story to be credible, but we cannot verify a primary source.[1]

Folklore suggests Fanny Margaret attended the Emma Willard School for girls in Middlebury, but Willard began teaching in 1807, and by that time, Fanny Margaret was 23. As a young woman, she became engaged to be married and was sincerely in love. Nonetheless, for various reasons debated by historians but unknown, much to the dismay of her mother, Fanny, and stepfather Jabez Penniman, she entered a convent in the Religious Hospitallers of St. Joseph at the Hotel Dieu in Montreal. At the time, there were no Catholic churches in Vermont. One account of her "veiling ceremony" after three years of training is attributed to her friend, Laura Jacob, from Westminster. Jacob and several of her friends from Middlebury traveled to Montreal to witness her ceremony.[2]

Jacob's account described a group of nuns with lighted tapers and the novice Fanny entering the chapel with a taper ornamented with flowers, chanting a dirge, kneeling, and attending a mass and a sermon. The Abbess led her to a wicket, where Fanny Margaret received her vows. The priest ratified them with a ring for her to wear until death. The ring was a passport to St. Peter. She then received the holy sacrament from the priest. The novice prostrated herself on the earth, covered by a pall, and was supported by four nuns who knelt beside her.

The priest who conducted the solemn ceremony spoke in French and read the "Burial Service for the Dead." The nuns performed a long chant that called on the holy saints to bless and protect her. The priest then replaced Fanny's white veil with a black one and placed a crown of flowers upon it. The veil and flowers were to be kept and worn to the grave and accompany her to immortality. Fanny Margaret then walked around the chapel with her taper and saluted each of her sister nuns. She then sat next to the superior and joined in a solemn chant, which closed the ceremony.

Sister Fanny Allen served as a nurse in the War of 1812 in Burlington's military hospital. At that time, the military base, including a hospital, was in present-day Battery Park. Some say Fanny was the first Catholic nun in New England. According to Jacob and others, she had many visitations from others; Sister Fanny Allen was admired and beloved for her beauty and grace in Montreal. As a nun from Vermont, which had no Catholic churches at the time, and as a daughter of Ethan Allen, she was a novelty. Fanny Margaret became sick with a lung disease, possibly tuberculosis, and predeceased her mother, Fanny Allen Penniman, in 1819. The church buried her in Montreal.[3,4]

Long after her death, the Edmundites of Montreal donated money to fund a hospital in Colchester bearing Fanny Allen's name. In 1894, the Edmundites founded the Fanny Allen Hospital Hotel Du Dieu on the Dunbars Hotel site. The land is the former Penniman farm, where Fanny lived while growing up. Today, the Fanny Allen Hospital is part of the UVM Health Network.

Many people wonder about the paradox of Ethan, an outspoken church critic, fathering a child who devoted her life to the church. Historians note that Fanny and Jabez were Diests, as well as their attorneys Udney Hay and Stephen Rowe Bradley. What combination of nature and nurture prompted Fanny's path in life? What would Ethan have thought or said? Although there is a folklore story that teases and dramatizes the question at this point, there is very little primary documentation that would illuminate her path into Catholicism.

Fanny and Ethan's first son, Hannibal Montresor Allen, married Agnes Bodine Low in 1808 when he was only 21, the same year Fanny and Jabez put the brakes on 19-year-old Ethan Alphonso's marital plans. We don't know if Fanny and Jabez held Hannibal to the same scrutiny with his marital life as they did with his brother Ethan Alphonso. Hannibal passed away in 1813 at 25, while still working for the Army. It is unknown if he and his wife had children.

Fanny and Ethan's second son, Captain Ethan Alphonso Allen, born in Burlington eight months after his father's death, enjoyed a 12-year military career and a long, prosperous life. In 1817, Captain Allen married Mary Susanna Johnston. Mary died the following year. Allen's second wife was Martha Washington Johnston, the sister of his first wife Susanna, and they enjoyed a long life together. Martha died the same year he did, in 1855, in Norfolk, Virginia. They produced two children, Ethan Alphonso, Jr. and Mary Robertine. Ethan and Martha are both buried in Elmwood Cemetery in Burlington.[5]

Captain Ethan Alphonso Allen, USA, 1819, Oil on mahogany, 21 x 19 1/8 inches (53.3 x 48.5 cm), son of Ethan Allen and Fanny Montresor Allen.

William Dunlap, American, 1766-1839), Chrysler Museum of Art, Norfolk VA.

One of Ethan Allen's daughters with Mary Brownson, Lucy Caroline, married attorney Samuel Hitchcock (1755-1813) in April 1789, shortly after Ethan died. We can imagine a wedding and reception at the Ethan Allen Homestead on the river in Burlington. They lived in Burlington for several years, then moved to Vergennes, where several of their children were born. As noted before, Hitchcock was a prominent attorney and public servant in Vermont. Ethan Allen had a healthy respect for Hitchcock and likely approved of his courtship and marriage to his daughter Lucy.

Hitchcock served as an attorney for Ira and Levi Allen, a justice of the peace, Vermont's first attorney general, a U.S. district court judge, and a member of the Vermont Assembly. Their children who lived to adulthood included Lorraine Allen (born in 1790), Henry (1792), MaryAnn (1796), Ethan Allen (1798), and Samuel (1805).[6]

Lorraine, Lucy Caroline Hitchcock's oldest child, married George P.

Peters in 1814, the year after Judge Hitchcock died. But Lorraine passed away the following year. Lorraine's obituary on May 5, 1815, in the *Vermont Gazette* remembered her. "She was a young lady of the most brilliant talents, elegant in her manners and amiable in her disposition. In her, society has lost one of its brightest ornaments, and her connexions, one of the lovliest of friends."[7]

Ethan Allen Hitchcock
Public domain.

Henry (1792-1839), the Hitchcocks' second child, graduated from the University of Vermont. He borrowed $300 from a neighbor, repaid it a year later, and traveled to Alabama Territory. There, Henry studied law, helped write the Alabama Constitution, became Alabama Attorney General, and in 1835 was appointed Chief Justice of the Alabama Supreme Court. Judge Henry Hitchcock died of yellow fever and left his wife Anne Erwin with five young children.[8]

Another one of Lucy Caroline and Samuel Hitchcock's children reached even greater status. According to Lucy, her son, Ethan Allen Hitchcock (1798-1870), bore a strong resemblance to his grandfather, General Ethan Allen. Ethan Allen Hitchcock was born almost 10 years after Ethan passed away and wouldn't have had the chance ever to know any of his grandfather's siblings. However, he would have known his Grandmother Fanny well, his slightly older aunt, Fanny Margaret, uncles Hannibal and Ethan Alphonso, and other kin who lived into the 1800s.

After a long military career, General Ethan Allen Hitchcock waited to marry until he was 70, only two years before his death. He was an intellectual philosopher who wrote books on topics ranging from the occult to Swedenborgianism to a theoretical interpretation of

Shakespeare's sonnets. As if that wasn't enough, he dabbled in alchemy. His military career was exemplary but complicated.

General Hitchcock refused commands under Generals Grant and McClellan in the Union Army during the Civil War because of his advanced age. His biographer, Bernard Cohen, said he put his career at risk arguing against the fraudulent treatment of American Indians, which was not a popular view then. Hitchcock became a Union Army General and was one of President Lincoln's advisors during the Civil War. He wrote about military history and completed a memoir titled *Fifty Years in Camp and Field*, which narrates much of the Allen family history.[9]

Lucy Caroline Hitchcock would become notorious for moving back to Burlington from Alabama with two enslaved servants, Lavinia and Francis Parker, a mother and her son. Lucy Caroline Hitchcock freed Lavinia and Francis Parker after Lavinia's husband, Edward Parker, paid a manumission fee.[10,11]

The Family of Samuel Hitchcock and Lucy Caroline Allen Hitchcock:

Samuel Hitchcock (1755-1813) married (1789) Lucy Caroline Allen(1768-1842)

Lorraine Allen Hitchcock (1790-1815) married (1814) George P. Peters (1789-1819)

Henry Hitchcock (1792-1839) married Anne Erwin (1803-1854)

Samuel Hitchcock (1794-1806)

Mary Anne Hitchcock (1796-1823) married JSW Parkin (1793-1866)

Ethan Allen Hitchcock (1798-1870) married (1888) Martha Nichols[12]

IV

Allen's Legacy and Questions That Remain

19

The Question of Allen's Servants

Therefore, no male person, born in this country, or brought from over sea,[sic] ought to be holden by law, to serve any person, as a servant, slave, or apprentice, after he arrives to the age of twenty-one years; nor female, in like manner, after she arrives to the age of eighteen years, unless they are bound by their own consent, after they arrive to such age, or bound by law for the payment of debts, damages, fines, costs, or the like.

– Chapter 1, Vermont Constitution, 1777[1]

Two frequently asked questions at the Ethan Allen Homestead Museum include: Did the Allens enslave people? And, what relationship did the Allens have with the institution of slavery? Ethan Allen's biographies haven't directly addressed and reliably responded to these questions.

To answer, we need to look at primary source evidence. Henry Collins worked for Ethan Allen in Burlington. Collins' father, Captain John Collins, boarded Ethan's family at his inn on Battery Street for three months before the Allens moved into their house on the intervale in Burlington.

As part of the Ethan Allen memorial during the 1850s, Collins recalled, "Part of his [Ethan's] family, particularly his laborers, two negro men and a woman, were staying at the farm."

Today, the dictionary defines "laborers" as people doing unskilled, manual work for wages. But today's definition is different than in the past. When Collins offered his interview in 1858, laborers and servants could mean paid or unpaid workers. Moreover, we don't know if Collins knew their status and where they were on the spectrum of servitude.[2,3]

Ethan's wife, Fanny, was quoted as saying that she had paid sundry persons employed as carpenters and laborers when Ethan died and that she paid at least some of their wages in cloth. During the post-war financial crisis, when cash was scarce, employers paid laborers with goods, such as cloth, which they would make into clothing. This scenario may have been the case, but it doesn't prove or disprove whether the Allens were enslavers.[4]

In 1779, Allen wrote *A Vindication of the Opposition of the Inhabitants of Vermont to the Government of New York, and of Their Right to Form an Independent State*, a narrative that repudiated New York's claims to land in the Grants and declared Vermont settlers exempt from New York claims and taxes. In his book, Allen condemned slavery as immoral, unnatural, and unjust.

However, some scholars have faulted Allen with disparaging enslaved people in *Vindication*, when he conflated the abomination of human enslavement with the political enslavement of Grants settlers by New York's landlords. This view says Allen further divided Black people and White poeple in America by denigrating the former. Allen's views on the institution of enslavement seem clear. Nonetheless, people's views about slavery were and are complex. Did his actions in his personal life match the words of his professional life? *Vindication* doesn't answer that question.[5,6]

In a letter written to his slave-owning brother and merchant Levi in St. John, Quebec, Ethan asked Levi to "send winter cloth and shoes" for his "Negroes" at the farm. Levi must have encountered Ethan's Black workers and knew roughly their sizes for clothing and shoes. The use of the word Negroes, which nowadays is offensive, could have referred to both enslaved or free Black people. Even if Allen's Black workers were freed laborers who worked for wages, why would Ethan single out the Black workers from the White workers? Were they treated differently than the White employees, or is there another explanation?[7]

Hawley Witters claimed to have worked on the Allen farm in 1788 and identified one of the Black laborers as "Newport." Although single names were often the hallmark of enslaved Black people, we don't know if Black men and women who were free customarily adopted first and last names to note their freedom or if they kept their single names. Witters' quote is a first-person account that raises the question of Newport's status, but it is inconclusive as proof of whether he was enslaved or free.[8]

In the same letter, Witters remembered Ethan always paying his workers on time, and Ira continued to pay them after Ethan passed away. Did all of Ethan's workers earn wages, or was Witters referring only to the wage earners and not the non-wage earners (if there were any)?

Finally, in an undated statement, Fanny Allen Penniman's granddaughter, Ellen Goodrich, suggested her Grandmother Penniman's Black housekeeper was the mother of "Eliza," a Black housekeeper who worked in the kitchen at the Pennimans and possibly for her parents, the Moodys. According to the Goodrich account, Eliza and her mother were "inherited." Some historians interpret this to mean the Pennimans inherited Eliza and her mother from the Ethan Allen Homestead. Others point out the lack of clarity in the account and the possibility they could have been inherited from the Walls, Jabez Penniman, or others. Could a free person be "inherited" from someone else? A deeper discussion on the Goodrich account follows.[9]

The most objective information about the Allens' laborers is the Collins affidavit and the Witters account. These statements tell us that three Black laborers worked at the Ethan Allen Homestead when Allen died on February 12, 1789. Based on Witters's account, the Black workers included two men and one woman, and one of the male farmhands was named Newport. The Collins and Witters accounts appear to be factual evidence but inconclusive.

The Collins Statement

Proof of whether or not the Allens enslaved people could hinge on Henry Collins's statement, which is inconclusive. Allen scholars John Duffy and Nick Muller in *Inventing Ethan Allen* insinuated that Allen had supervised enslaved people in the 1760s Connecticut lead mine. While this is possible, no evidence shows that this is true or that enslaved people or indentured servants worked for any of the Allen siblings other than for Ethan's brother Levi.

One of Levi's surviving letters and a reward he posted in the Hartford Courant for Prince, his enslaved man, is conclusive. Later on, after Prince was captured, Levi commented in correspondence that Prince was very capable, and he put his trust in him to run his store in St. John, Quebec, when he was away. The evidence of Levi's behavior is clear. But we find no clarity with the other Allens, including Ethan or Fanny. [10]

In a best-case scenario, the Allens employed White and Black servants and farmhands. They paid their workers wages and benefits based on their skills and experience and not their skin color. Their pay included clothing, board, and food if cash was unavailable.

In a worst-case scenario, Ethan and Fanny Allen employed people they owned as chattel. The workers were relatively powerless and dependent on the Allens. Even if they were free, they might not have felt free. Several factors complicate this question. There are no probate records, manumission statements, invoices, or receipts to add clarity. Many Black people had no records or paper trail. The lack of a definitive answer leaves ambiguity and unknowns surrounding their workers.

We know that Ethan Allen lived in a systemically racist and patriarchal world, and he associated with both slave-owning friends and acquaintances, as well as abolitionists such as Stephen Rowe Bradley, Moses Robinson, and Hector St. John de Crevecouer. Like most White leaders of his time, Allen was not a highly visible social activist or abolitionist. Scholar Michael Bellesiles, who researched and wrote his 1987 Ph.D. dissertation on the life of Ethan Allen, claimed Allen was angry that his brother Levi had bought Prince, the enslaved man. Unfortunately, we can't verify this. [11]

Vindication?

However inconclusive the statements of associates and eyewitnesses were, and the filtered interpretation of their semantics in hindsight, we do know how Allen felt about the institution of slavery. Allen wrote in his pointed *Vindication* book that fighting for freedom was preferable to submitting to slavery. Allen referred to New York Governor Clinton, who solicited support from the Continental Congress to take New York's side in the conflict with Vermont. Clinton threatened to send armed troops into Vermont territory to enforce New York patents. Here is a paragraph from Allen's book.

"FROM fifteen years acquaintance with the government of New-York,[sic] Vermont is by no means willing to trust this important controversy to their decision of justice and equity, as it has hitherto deviated from every idea of those rules of moral rectitude which are practised by virtuous governments; their notions of justice and equity seem to be unnatural and unjust; at least, every sample of it which they have as yet exhibitted to those inhabitants appears to be so; probably a habit of inslaving their subjects has beat it into their heads, that it is just; and thus people commonly conceive it to be just to enslave *Negroes*."[sic][12]

Notwithstanding Allen's convoluted prose, there is no doubt about it: Allen said New York's principles of justice and equity toward Vermont were unnatural, unjust, and morally wrong. He stated that habitual enslavement and "beating it into their heads" might have convinced them that imposed slavery was "just." Allen's paragraph sounds like he believed enslavement was unjust.

The above statement is the most direct assertion Allen made about enslavement. He indicated he believed enslaving Black people is wrong.

Allen's argument that political slavery was no more justified than chattel slavery shows a disdain for life-long enslavement. However, his stated belief does not clarify his relationships with his workers or whether or not he enslaved people. Unfortunately, according to Black history scholars, Allen's rhetoric has a negative impact.

For example, scholar Harvey Amani Whitfield points out that when Allen used inflammatory words like "slavery" or "enslaved," it fired up his supporters. In Whitfield's words, "Some members of Vermont's leadership held disparaging views of enslaved people that depicted them as the opposite of virtuous, honorable, and autonomous Patriots. These stereotypes made equality between Blacks and Whites unlikely, as local Whites had been virtuous in defense of their rights, while African Americans had allegedly accepted their lowly place." Whitfield maintains that enslaved people were regarded as the antithesis of Vermont's courageous White backcountry population. Instead, they were a degraded group, a servant class, who were not ready for citizenship or equality.[13]

According to Whitfield, Allen's persistent portrayals of political and chattel slavery disparaged enslaved Black people and equated slavery with timidity and poverty. Since the choice Allen offered in his rhetoric was freedom or slavery, the implication was that to be free, Vermonters needed to be courageous, as the founders had been, lest they become indolent enslaved people. In Whitfield's view, Allen's rhetoric further separated Black and White people in Vermont.

The Goodrich Account

What might have happened to the Allens' workers after Allen died in 1789? Within a year, Fanny had moved back to Westminster to live with her aunt Margaret and her husband, Patrick Wall. If the Allen's Black housekeeper mentioned by Henry Witters had been working for the Allen family in Burlington, did she and the Allens' Black male laborers continue to live with and work for Fanny? The 1791 census doesn't indicate that Black people lived in the Fanny Allen home in

Burlington or the Wall household in Westminster at that time. Unfortunately, census data was not always accurate or reliable. And the Goodrich account raises other questions.

The Goodrich essay is cryptic and confusing. It's an account of Fanny Allen Penniman's granddaughter, Ellen Moody Goodrich (1840-1917), who went by the name of Mrs. John E. Goodrich. Goodrich's husband, UVM Latin professor and librarian John E. Goodrich (1831-1913), is said to have written the two-page "Reminiscences" essay based on Ellen's girlhood memories. No other documents from Ellen Goodrich survive. This account described an older Black woman who worked in her grandmother Penniman's kitchen.[14]

The undated Goodrich essay is a faded two-page typed mimeograph copy on tissue paper in the Allen Family Papers in the UVM Special Collections Library. It touches on various topics, including Grandmother Fanny Allen Penniman's graceful style, her voluminous reading, and book collections. It was written whimsically, didn't offer clear facts, and does not have the validity of original primary source documents that are handwritten, published, signed, dated, sworn statements, or otherwise authenticated. The paragraph below concerns the servants at Grandmother Fanny Penniman's home. It was written in language that is today considered to be racially insensitive and offensive.

"The servants of that household used to grow up in the house with the family. The old darkey cook that we loved to hear about was the mother of our inherited "queen of the food-land," as we named her. She would keep the children chained to her sides whole evenings, telling all sorts of strange weird tales. Rolling her eyes and swaying her head, she would break forth into wild strains of melody, with unknown words; and the music, unearthly as it was, impressed these little listeners, filling their hearts with a kind of veneration akin to reverence. Yes, even our old Black Eliza did all these entertaining performances in a less fashion, to our great edification; and there still hangs about that tall gaunt dark woman a flavor of mystery. We all loved her in a way. She was a part of our life, —to be cared for, to be nursed, if sick, to the very end, with gentleness and patience, 'be she never so graceless or wicked.'"[15]

Cringeworthy and racist words like "old darkey cook" trigger images today of an enslaved woman. And entertaining the children with singing and strange, weird tales for hours conjures up unpleasant stereotypes today, at the very least. But it doesn't tell us if she was free or enslaved. This account also suggests but doesn't confirm multigenerational kitchen help in the Fanny Allen Penniman kitchen. Can the timeframe help us understand the context of this account?

The narrator, Ellen Moody Goodrich, was the daughter of Adelia Penniman Moody (1801-1884), the youngest daughter of Jabez and Fanny Allen Penniman. Did Fanny or Adelia pass down some or all of the memories in the essay? Did Ellen Moody Goodrich have these experiences during her childhood?

Ethan Allen (1738-1789) - Fanny Montresor Allen (1760-1839) -
Jabez Penniman (1764-1841)
Adelia Penniman (1801-1884)- Dr Moody (1801-1841))
Ellen Moody Goodrich (1840-1917) - John E. Goodrich (1831-1913)

Ellen Moody Goodrich was born a year after Grandmother Fanny Penniman had died. Adelia would have had to be at least five or 10 years old to have been able to remember the Black woman who worked in the Penniman kitchen, and the Pennimans had left the Ethan Allen Homestead by 1800. Therefore, if Ellen Goodrich recounted an eyewitness account from her mother, Adelia, the story would date from 1807 to 1811, when the Penniman home was in Colchester. This time frame would have been 17 to 22 years after Ethan died in 1789. But there are other questions about the reminiscences.[16]

When Goodrich stated, "Even our old Black Eliza did all these entertaining performances in a lesser fashion," she alluded to the possibility that Eliza's mother had also entertained the kids at Penniman's kitchen. Suppose Eliza, an older Black woman, was the daughter of the unnamed older Black woman who worked for the Pennimans. In that case, the time frame puts Eliza's service with the Pennimans during the early to mid-19th century.

But more questions arise: From whom did Goodrich hear these stories about the old Black woman? From whom did the Pennimans "inherit" Eliza and her mother? We don't know. Although some readers will assume that Goodrich was talking about inheriting Eliza and her mother from the Ethan Allen Homestead kitchen in Burlington, Eliza and her mother, if they were free or in bondage, could have been inherited from the Walls, the prior bachelor Jabez Penniman, or others.

When folklore is repeated enough, it takes on credibility. Some historians mistakenly named the Allens' housekeeper Eliza, presumably not reading the Goodrich account closely, even though Goodrich's character would have lived a generation later than the Allens did in Burlington. Eliza and her mother might have had the same name, but there is no evidence. The Goodrich essay does not establish that Eliza or her mother lived at the homestead in 1788.

The more we attempt to interpret the information available in sources, the less definitive it becomes. If Eliza's mother did work for the Allen family at the homestead, and the Pennimans inherited her, does that strengthen the possibility that they enslaved her? Fanny Allen's next husband, Jabez Penniman, could have inherited an enslaved woman and her daughter from Fanny through couverture laws. If Eliza or her mother worked for the Allens, they could have continued working for wages with the Penniman family. Regardless of the workers' status, Goodrich's language and imagery reveal condescension and prejudice. Systemic prejudice was prevalent during the 18th and 19th centuries and in the Allen, Penniman, Moody, and Goodrich families.

When we examine the Goodrich essay critically, factually, and logically, we have unanswered questions about who wrote it, when, their state of mind, and who they were talking about. It tells us nothing conclusive about workers at the Ethan Allen homes in Sunderland or Burlington. The Goodrich reminiscence doesn't answer these questions.

The 1777 Vermont Constitution asserted that no person ought to serve as a servant, slave, or apprentice in Vermont for males 21 and over and females 18. According to historian Elise Guyette, Black people of all ages were still openly and secretly enslaved and reenslaved for many decades in the Green Mountain State. The wording of "ought" instead of "shall" kept the 1777 constitution from abolishing slavery outright. The Vermont Constitution also permitted the enslavement of minors. Guyette says the reason for that was the White belief that "Black parents were unable to bring up their children properly, and they needed a White guiding hand." They just ignored the constitution that said they ought not to be enslaved. In fact, in 1800, a Vermont Supreme Court Justice, Stephen Jacob, was let off the hook by the Vermont Supreme Court for enslaving a woman for 17 years and not caring for her after she became blind and destitute later in life. How could this happen?[17]

Vermont's constitution attempted to abolish adult slavery a few years before Massachusetts (1783), and Connecticut (1784) did the same. And Vermont closed the "ought" loophole to the legally binding "shall" in 1784. But in each case, conditions or loopholes existed that allowed the enslavement of minors or freedom for those born after a specific date, keeping those born before the date enslaved for life or living under other conditional enslavement scenarios. Enslavers from Massachusetts and Maine served in the U.S. Congress as late as the 1800s. The institution of enslavement thrived in New York, Connecticut, and other northern colonies, not to mention across the American South.

In Vermont, based on the 1791 Census, it is possible that there were at least scores of Black people who were enslaved within the state borders. Guyette says even though the census listed many Black people as free or "other persons," those people were almost certainly enslaved. Ethan Allen and many of the Vermont settlers had grown up in Connecticut and Massachusetts during a time when enslavement had been commonplace among the middle class as well as affluent people. Connecticut had the largest slave population per capita in the northern colonies.[18,19]

Professor Jared Hardesty at Western Washington University suggested looking closely at the Allens' account books, receipts, inventory lists, and probate records that might mention enslaved people, as they could appear as property in those accounts. "After about 1720 or so, New Englanders stopped including indentured servants in probate inventories and would only include enslaved people. If you find them in a probate inventory, they were without question enslaved." None of Ethan or Fanny's account books, receipts, inventory lists, or probate records found so far indicate or mention enslaved people.[20]

None of the Allen siblings' wills or inventory lists included enslaved people, as noted in Heman's, Heber's, and Zimri's biographies. Ethan's probate and inventory list of the Allen house in Burlington only consisted of a handful of small personal items when it was completed and recorded by Fanny's attorney, Udney Hay. Looking farther back at the historical records of Woodbury and Cornwall, Connecticut, gives us more insight into 18th-century circumstances.

Institutionalized Slavery

The History of Ancient Woodbury, where Ethan worked and his first wife Mary Brownson Allen was born and raised, has this to say about the institution of slavery.

"All the leading men and men of property, in the early days, owned slaves. The fact is attested by all our records, town, probate and ecclesiastical. ... During the whole of the eighteenth century, the institution flourished here, though in a mild form. The various records show, that a considerable proportion of the personal estate of the more opulent of the inhabitants consisted of negro servants." By 1774, half of all the ministers, lawyers, & public officials, and a third of all the doctors enslaved people. But, according to this account, Connecticut's large slave population was based in the middle class.[21]

The author of "Ancient Woodbury," William Cothren, noted that in 1784, the Connecticut legislature began the gradual abolition of enslavement in stages. First, they abolished slavery for specific age groups, then the transportation of enslaved people. They required the registration of newborns to account for their eventual emancipation, and so on. It is doubtful there was the prosecution of illegal enslavement or trafficking at that time. During the 1700s, there were examples of groups of up to 60 enslaved people working on thousand-acre plantations in

Connecticut. Slavery was the "powerhouse" of the economy, more so in the South, but even in parts of Connecticut. But by the end of the 18th century, less than four percent of people in Connecticut were Black, and many of them were free, according to researcher Joel Lang.[22]

Connecticut kept a registry of violent or untimely deaths for enslaved people between the years of 1711 and 1892. Most of the names of enslaved victims in the index have surnames, which often were the surnames of their owners. The 60 untimely deaths reported between 1738 and 1776 included drowning, hanging, "accidents with a large stone," shooting, and other scenarios. The surnames of Allen or Brownson don't appear on that index or other indexes that might verify that either family was an enslaver. Other small Connecticut towns were similar to Woodbury.[23]

Ethan lived in neighboring Cornwall and Northampton, Massachusetts, for a while. *The History of Northampton* mentions White people enslaving Indian people during the French and Indian War. Captured Indian children were boarded out from the town (by bids) to farmers. Researcher Ryan Bachman found that in Cornwall, "Slavery in the North was a different institution than it was in the South; "Slave and master might labor in the fields together, and the slave might eat at the farm table with the family, but he still did not have freedom." This scenario might have been a White perspective of institutionalized slavery in Cornwall during the Allens' time. But as Bachman noted, the underlying injustice of enslavement was always there.[24,25]

The Woodbury and Northampton histories mention a so-called "mild" form of slavery, compared to a more violent and brutal oppression that was more common in the southern states. This belief supported irrational thinking that some enslaved people were relatively "happy" with their place in life despite not having rights or freedom, let alone being owned by other human beings. White beliefs about the immorality of the institution gradually became stronger during the 18th century. Even so, the town histories noted there were still curfews, and authorities whipped Black people found outside after 9 PM.[26,27]

The historical research and commentaries from Woodbury, Cornwall, and Northampton offer a flavor of the 18th-century White view of the cultural environment in which Ethan and his siblings grew up, surrounded by heavily entrenched institutionalized slavery. For anyone living in Connecticut, enslavement was commonplace and normalized as a way of life, at least within the dominant White culture in which the Allens formed their values.

Gretchen Gerzina's book about Lucy Terry and her husband Abijah, *Mr. and Mrs. Prince: How an Extraordinary Eighteenth-Century Family Moved out of Slavery and Into Legend*, corroborates the notion that the enslavement in New England was different than in the South. Gerzina points out that enslaved people could learn to read and write, attend church, travel, marry, and even sue others in court. Some may calculate that it was incrementally better than the brutality of the South, but it was slim consolation. For one thing, as Gerzina points out, the despondence and isolation of the enslaved people often lead to suicides.

How strong was the abolitionist movement during the 1780s? Quakers and others boycotted white sugar (refined from slave plantations) but not maple sugar. It was not as if slave-free rum was identified, marketed, or widely available as fairtrade products are today. Enslaved people were forced to work on the sugar cane, cotton, and tobacco plantations regardless of whether they lived in the West Indies, the South, or the Northern colonies. There is no evidence that Allen or the general public bought free-trade rum, cotton, or tobacco if they could find it. There was sporadic antislavery writing and organizing during the 1700s before Allen died in 1789, but we don't see evidence that the Allens supported the abolition ideology. As participants in the economy that depended on slavery, Allen and his family and society participated in supporting the institution. There are other ways to view Allen's relationship with enslavement.[28]

Some of Allen's associates enslaved, and others emancipated Black people. The enslavers include Matthew Lyon, the former indentured servant; Stephen Fay, the owner of the Catamount Tavern; Benjamin Stiles, Allen's business partner of the Northampton lead mine; New York Loyalist Philip Skene; and, of course, Ethan's brother, Levi.[29]

On a more positive note, Allen's close friend and attorney Stephen Rowe Bradley proposed a bill in the U.S. Senate to ban imports of enslaved people in 1805. Ebenezer Allen, Ethan's fourth cousin, emancipated an enslaved woman in 1777. Allen's friend, Hector St. John, wrote about equality and joined a Paris antislavery organization, The Society of the Friends of the Blacks, in 1788.[30,31,32]

Bronze markers showing where Lavinia and Frances Parker were enslaved at the corner of Main and Lafayette Streets (presently Pine Street) by Lucy Caroline Allen Hitchcock.
Author photo

Although Allen did write thousands of pages of propaganda condemning the tyranny of the king's men in New York and a book on philosophy, none of his writings categorically repudiate the institution of slavery or servitude as a cause. While there was some abolitionist writing by White and Black people in the colonies, social activism in the dominant culture was not widespread then.

One high-profile example of enslavement in Vermont is Ethan's daughter, Lucy Caroline Hitchcock, who had moved to Alabama to live with her son, Henry Hitchcock. Henry was a successful attorney, businessman, and the wealthiest man in Alabama, and he enslaved several people. Lucy moved back to Burlington in 1835, along with 35-year-old Lavinia Parker and her legally enslaved son, Francis Parker. They labored for Hitchcock on present-day Main Street in downtown Burlington for at least several years. Lavinia's husband had to buy their freedom. Two small brass plaques on the Main Street sidewalk mark where they lived with Hitchcock.[33,34]

In many cases, the lines were blurred, and freedom or enslavement wasn't an either/or question. Scholar Jared Hardesty points out the uncertain status of many Black people at the time, particularly in the Maritime provinces. If Black people were not formally enslaved nor free, this allowed for a different, nefarious form of exploitation. In this scenario, enslavers could flourish without being accountable. Without formal emancipation and being "servants for life," Black people didn't have any legal power and wouldn't have rights that civilized society would ensure. In a free state, Black people could be de facto enslaved, without capital, resources, support, or opportunities to be genuinely free. [35,36]

Elise Guyette pointed out, "Housing patterns show that Blacks strived to live independent lives away from White households, but most did not succeed... Seldom were Black households headed by Black men or women." Black families often did not remain intact as a stable unit. People of color looking to build economic independence and freedom faced a challenging, if not impossible, proposition. [37]

Even the most objective evidence doesn't answer the question as to whether Ethan and Fanny owned enslaved people. This conclusion may be a disappointment for readers who want a definitive answer. But, as we have seen, there is no solid evidence, and the status of Black people in the 18th century was often complex and unclear. On the question of Allen's relationship with the institution of slavery, his values and opinions certainly would have affected the 1784 Vermont Constitution, which abolished adult slavery, but permitted the enslavement of children. There is no evidence that Allen was an antislavery activist, even though he had stated it was wrong, and like most White people, he appeared to acquiesce to cultural norms that surrounded him growing up. Researchers will continue to explore Allen's family, his Black laborers, and his relationship with the institution of slavery during his life to understand better and answer these questions.

20

Allen and the Indians

Note: For the purposes of this chapter, Abenaki citizen and author Joseph Bruchac confirms that "Indian" is the appropriate term to use when speaking about Indigenous peoples in the northeast.

We cannot know what Ethan Allen thought about living in the unceded homeland of Indigenous Peoples. Objective accounts are even less prevalent than with the questions about slavery. Early biographers attribute him to exploring the Grants wilderness to hunt, fish, and learn from his Indian friends, but with few primary source citations. Indians had lived seasonally and year-round in what is now Vermont for over 10,000 years. In most cases, the French and British governments and settlers assumed land ownership during colonization.

Abenaki campsite in Vermont.
Author photo

The Abenaki and other tribes endured the French and Indian War from 1754 to 1763, as well as the French and British colonial occupation of their homelands. The French and English had moved in and built mills in Swanton before 1780. Devastating European diseases wiped out tens of thousands, perhaps hundreds of thousands of Indians. By the 1770s, colonists streamed into the Grants, primarily from Connecticut and Massachusetts, bought grants from Governor Wentworth, pitched farms, and formed townships.

When the American Revolution erupted from 1775 to 1783, many of the Indians fled north to the vicinity of Montreal to avoid the conflict. Yet, hundreds of Indians from different northeast tribes fought alongside the northern British Army for General John Burgoyne. British-led attacks on early Vermont towns, often called "Indian raids," burned settlements. Settlers who fought back were killed, and prisoners were taken north to Canada. Often, the American prisoners served as enslaved people or indentured servants once they arrived in Canada. Although British General John Burgoyne instructed the Indian warriors not to commit atrocities or abuse women or children, there are accounts of women and children being kidnapped and killed. Vermonters were concerned about the Indian warriors, especially with British-led raids on the settlements.[1,2,3]

On May 14, 1775, Ethan Allen wrote an open appeal to the "Loving brothers and friends," Indians from the "Headquarters of the Army in Crown Point," asking for support against the British, who had waged war on America. He recommended Captain Abraham Ninham of Stockbridge, a well-known Indian ambassador of peace, to four Canadian tribes for help. Allen attempted to entice Indians to fight against the British, knowing that Burgoyne was recruiting them to fight alongside his army.

Allen said, "I was always a friend of the Indians and have hunted with them many times, and learned to shoot and ambush like Indians, and am a great hunter. I want to have your warriors come and see me, and help me fight the King's Regular troops." Allen asked the warriors to fight with him in the bush instead of rank and file as the British did. He offered his Indian brothers blankets, food, rum, bread, and venison.[4]

One has to wonder what Indians thought when, in the letter, Allen said Americans "have done you no wrong, and desire to live with you as brothers." He asked them not to fight for the British but to fight their common enemy, King George's British Army.[5]

Many of us today would take issue with Allen's claim that Americans had done the Indians no wrong. There must have been some resentment in the Indian community for the longstanding relentless colonization of their homeland in general. The offer of provisions and blankets by that time might have been unpalatable since settlers had infected Indians with diseased blankets, and hundreds of thousands of Indians across the northeast had been annihilated by European diseases by then. The Indian tribal communities had been decimated, depleted, and weakened by that point, and they were in no position to negotiate. There is one other Allen letter regarding the Indians that survives today.

Some Ethan Allen critics point to Allen's letter to American commander General Philip Schuyler on September 8, 1775, as an example of Allen's barbarity toward Indians. By then, the Revolutionary War raged with tens of thousands of British troops and hundreds of Indian Warriors under British command. British General Guy Carleton, governor of Quebec from 1768 to 1778, had tried to limit the participation of British aide Guy Johnson's Iroquois allies. Still, Colonel Ethan Allen and the American Patriots didn't know that.[6]

General Schuyler was preparing to fight the British Army, which had earlier employed hundreds of Indians to fight with them. In Allen's September 8, 1775 letter to Schuyler, one week before Allen was captured and imprisoned, Allen mentioned the Indian warriors. In his truncated letter, Allen shows his fear of the Indians, and despite the Canadians' neutrality, he hopes the Canadians will be Patriot allies.

Allen's letter to General Schuyler begins by saying savages pursued them and they managed to escape after they experienced "Extream Fatigue." Allen goes on to say:

"Yesterday the Indians Killed and scalped a Frenchman on the west side of the river, the Canadians Guard us Night and day and Took Great Courage at learning of the seige of Saint Johns, Captain Benedict and his Boat crew killed four Indians which were Burned at Saint Johns as we hear."[7]

The last page of the letter reads:

"The Indians have not engaged in the war as the Canadians tell us You Need Not fear the Canadians will rise against us their Cunning is to fight on Neither side but as we have worked our-Selves into their affections they we apprehend will fight for our Safety and we hope to Excite a number to Cut off the communication between Saint Johns, Chamblee and Montreal, be this as it will. Nutrality on their part with Gods Blessing and a Competency of economy and Courage I should think would Insure you Saint Johns, we are Told the Indians murmer against the regular [British Army] on account of their slain as they urged them into the war, the more you kill of them the Better, Exchange of Life for Toys they find to be unequal, I am Obt. S...
To The General Schuyler" [8]

Some modern historians and social activists have said Ethan's statement, "The more you kill of them, the Better," showed a character flaw. Other historians read Allen's passage as telling Schuyler the Indians' attitude was the more British you kill, the better, since the British were the ones who urged the Indians into war. Either way, the context of active military wartime engagement might provide a better understanding of what the letter meant than one sentence alone. Ethan's brother Ira has a less ambiguous record of his treatment of the Indians. [9]

Ira's autobiography recounts how he, Remember Baker, Issac Vanornum, and others (Ethan was not present) confronted a New York surveyor named John Stevens, his party, and a dozen Indians on the banks of the Onion River in the early 1770s. After holding Stevens at gunpoint, Ira told him to leave and that he would kill him if he ever saw him again. Allen then used Vanornum, who had been held captive by the Indians and knew their language, to tell the Indians that it was only a property dispute between the two White men and it had nothing to do with them. He assured them they would be free to hunt and fish on those lands and waters as they pleased. The Indians stayed in their canoe and went on their way.[10]

By the 1780s, Ira took a more hostile stance against the Indians in Swanton, a Vermont town on the Canada border. Before the war, the Abenakis had lived in Swanton and other areas in Vermont for thousands of years. There is ample oral tradition and archeological evidence to that effect. When the war broke out, a population of Abenaki in the Swanton area moved north into Canada to remove themselves from the conflict between Great Britain and the American settlers. Many of the Indians had endured the French and Indian War and were not interested in being involved in military strife again.[11]

However, during that time, Ira acquired most of the town of Swanton. At the end of the war during the 1780s, many Indians returned to their prior homes in Swanton to find a burgeoning European settlement in their homeland. Not surprisingly, there were some disputes and protests by the Indians. Upon hearing of altercations and raids disrupting the settlers in Swanton, Ira sent in the state militia to get control of the situation, and it didn't end well for the Indians. Ira effectively removed perceived troublemakers, resulting in an oppressive situation for the Abenaki tribe that had lived there long before the Europeans arrived. [12]

Ethan may not have been directly involved in Ira's oppression and subjugation of Indians during peacetime. Still, as a land speculator and business partner in the ORLC, he was party to their treatment and part of the systemic appropriation of their mostly unceded land in Vermont.

21

Allen's Imprint on Vermont's Unique DNA 1770 - Today

Vermonters who have lived elsewhere know that our state has a unique ethos entirely different from most other states. Vermont still has a relatively small population and sparsely settled municipalities. Our landscape is spectacular, and we take care of it and cherish its natural beauty. We lean into long winters, enjoy the mountain ranges that split the state down the middle, and make the most of the border with Canada. There is a long history of multiethnic immigration in Burlington, although we are still racially homogenous compared to other states. Vermont has a complex political landscape as well.

The Green Mountain State is known for its paradoxically conservative tradition and progressive values. Because of our relatively small population, Vermont has more state representation per capita than other states: one state senator per 21,000 people, and one U.S. senator per 325,000 people, which gives individuals and groups significantly more access to political power than in most other states. Some unique and lasting characteristics, such as our geography and climate, seem beyond our control, and some were forged before and during the revolution. Ethan Allen and the Green Mountain Boys coded Vermont's original DNA, the distinct character of Vermont.[1]

Its distinctiveness should not be conflated with exceptionalism. Vermont is not necessarily exceptional or better than other states. Vermont possesses numerous unremarkable, ordinary, and limiting attributes. If we look at Vermont and its beginnings objectively, we see similarities with a few other states in the Union, but we find uniqueness that traces back to our beginnings.

Ethan Allen possessed a rare combination of traits during a singular time that coincided with an opportunity to shape the future. His charismatic influence rose to prominence by leading the Bennington paramilitary group that became known as the Green Mountain Boys. In 1770, they coalesced around defending their New Hampshire grant titles against the claims of the steady stream of New York governors and their associates. His so-called club law was admired by some and despised by others.

In 1775, as the leader of the Green Mountain Boys, Allen became the co-hero of Fort Ticonderoga and Crown Point, the first attack on the King's property. This event resulted in American cannons positioned on Dorchester Heights and the evacuation of the British from Boston, General Washington's first victory of the American Revolution. In 1780, Allen negotiated to end British-led raids on Grants towns terrorizing the settlers.

Biographer Michael Bellisles portrays Allen and the Green Mountain Boys as "a unifying symbol with the weight of enforcement." They filled an "activist core.... Allen worked hard to equate his faction's leadership with the existence of Vermont."[2]

Recent Vermont scholars point out that Allen subsequently botched an attack on St. John, and his peers chose Seth Warner over him for command of what became Warner's Regiment. The British subsequently captured him and most of his company in Montreal, and he spent 32 months in British confinement as a prisoner of war. These scholars also note that Allen and the Green Mountain Boys refused to acknowledge New York's rule of law and land claims in Vermont's territory to defend their purchased New Hampshire land grants. It is plausible that if they had acknowledged New York's rule of law, Vermont territory would now be counties in the northeastern arm of the Empire State.

Some historians have criticized Allen and the Boys for their some-times violent responses to armed New York reprisals and Loyalist settle-ments in the Grants territory. In some cases, the Green Mountain Boys, also called "the Mob," behaved like a terrorist organization against the Yorkers. According to some historians, New York authorities burned Grants settlers' houses and forcibly evicted Grants settlers. In one case, a Loyalist, Colonel John Reid, led an armed contingent of Scottish immigrants to settle in New Haven (present-day Vergennes) at the falls. It is well-substantiated that in response to Loyalist threats and violence perpetrated by New York sheriffs and posses, the Boys evicted settlers, burned houses, and held kangaroo courts to convict Loyalists of crimes during the 18th century. While charges the Green Mountain Boys used strong-arm tactics are sometimes valid, historians should view Allen's actions in the historical context of the rebellion and wartime milieu in which they occurred. In some cases, the Boys were reacting to violent attacks by New York posses. Their decisive responses and a strategy of quick, aggressive actions ultimately stymied New York aristocrats, their sheriffs, and posses.[3,4]

Legal scholar Gary Shattuck contends that Allen was a thug. On the other hand, Allen biographer Michael Bellesiles says, in the context of politics, rebellion, and war, "Allen was a bully who routinely used his size to cower others; he was 'our thug.' He routinely did the best he could for the people of Vermont to keep violence away from their homes, which strikes me as a significant accomplishment." Allen's polit-ical activism was more violent than Vermont's local activism today.[5,6,7]

The Bennington militia and "Boys" evolved out of a need to protect their New Hampshire Grants titles from being nullified, having to pay quitrents and confirmation fees, or keep from being evicted. One may wonder how the Boys could stay organized and influential in an inherently disorganized area without the rule of law and ready access to goods, printing presses, or other communication. Ethan and Ira Allen deserve a lot of credit for their communication and persuasive essays that influenced a lot of Vermonters and discouraged Loyalists during the 1770s and 1780s.

Allen also wrote a best-selling popular narrative of his experience in British captivity. Later, in 1784, as a self-styled philosopher, Allen boldly published *Reason*, based on his philosophy of using reason to explain life instead of religious doctrine at a time when the church had enormous power and influence in communities, colonies, and countries. He worked for years to establish Vermont as the 14th colony. When that failed, he worked to protect Vermont from attack, even when it meant negotiating with Great Britain and the Continental Congress simultaneously. Vermonters were depressed by the economic conditions and polarized between Loyalist and Patriot allegiance; some historians criticize Allen for negotiating with the British after the war. There is strong evidence that the Allens weren't interested in an alliance with Britain as much as they were interested in independence and advancing their financial goals.

Captain Heman Allen's widow, Abigail Wadhams, quoted Ethan Allen saying when Abigail's daughter, Lucinda, turned 18, her land inheritance from Heman would be worth more if Vermont remained independent instead of becoming a state. Kevin Graffagnino, an esteemed Ira Allen scholar, sums up the Allen brothers' motives this way: "We have a fair amount of evidence that Ethan, Ira, and Levi did not think statehood was a good idea in the late 1780s and early 1790s; understandable from their perspective, tied as they were to building a profitable water-borne trade with Canada. Ira gave up in January '91 and voted for statehood at the Bennington convention, but everyone who's ever looked at it has agreed that he went along because he knew it was a done deal rather than because he had changed his mind. For the Allens, independent Vermont had much greater potential for favorable trade arrangements with British Canada than Vermont as a state following trade agreements negotiated at a national level." [8,9]

The Green Mountain Boys' paramilitary actions were unlawful, based on New York's and other laws. As legal scholar Gary Shattuck said, "The assertion of Bennington authorities in 1772 that they had obstructed New York after the ejectment trials because of Allen's claim to 'Laws of Self and Family Preservation' is a decidedly deficient explanation to justify their actions in the context of established law. However, it does reveal the outlines of the alternative argument founded in equity, which it incorporated in its support, their strong, centuries-long New England traditions and institutions." [10]

Thuggish behavior and club law do not describe Vermont's ethos today, nor has it since the 18th century. But it was one tool that Allen and the Boys used to keep the New York authorities from enforcing their will on the Grants settlers and early Vermont. The other method Allen used was controlling the narrative.

The Power of the Pen

Ethan Allen enthusiasts often point to two reasons for his fame. As noted above, he is famous for his successful capture of Fort Ticonderoga and second for his authorship of two books: *A Narrative of Col. Ethan Allen's Captivity...*, and his Deist book on philosophy, *Reason the Only Oracle of Man: Or, A Compenduous System of Natural Religion* (*Reason*). But the sometimes overlooked justification of his importance is that Ethan and his brother Ira wrote thousands of pages of persuasive essays, books, pamphlets, broadsides, and op-ed pieces that advocated for Vermont independence and independent thinking. A few of Ethan's influential propaganda works include:

- *A Brief Narrative of the Proceedings of the Government of New York, Relative to Their Obtaining the Jurisdiction of That Large District of Land*, to the Westward from Connecticut River, 1774 (211 pages).
- "An Animadversory Address to the Inhabitants of the State of Vermont", 1778 (24 pages).
- *A Vindication of the Opposition of the Inhabitants of Vermont to the Government of New York, and of Their Right to Form an Independent Government*, 1779 (179 pages).

- *Narrative of Col. Ethan Allen's Captivity: Written by Himself,* 1780 (152 pages).
- "A Concise Refutation of the Claims of New Hampshire and Massachusetts Bay to the Territory of Vermont", with Jonas Fay, 1780 (29 pages).

This list does not include the dozens of personal notes, open letters, and public opinion pieces published in newspapers during his life or his appendix to *Reason*, which was published posthumously during the 1850s. For example, as late as November 30, 1784, Allen wrote a letter to the public updating Vermonters that he was persistently lobbying and negotiating with New York and Congress to "respect the independency of Vermont." Allen's ultimate aim was to win statehood, and he acknowledged that if admitted, Vermont would upset the balance of power with the southern (pro-slave) states. He noted the state was in respectable condition, Vermont courts do impartial justice, and "our citizens support the honor and dignity of our laws and unitedly combine to support our liberty and independency." [11]

Allen's published pieces before his imprisonment in 1775 impacted Vermont's thinking about its declaration of independence from the New York, New Hampshire, and Massachusetts colonies two years later. Allen's thinking and writing also influenced Vermont's constitution, which was written and adopted in 1777 while he was still imprisoned. Each of Allen's written pieces was conceived and written by hand, taken to a printing press to be printed, and then disseminated. Only one, *Reason*, was printed in Vermont. During the early to mid-1770s, the closest printer was in Hartford, Connecticut, which required several days of travel each way. Note that some of his monographs numbered at least 24 pages, and others were books. But they weren't only impressive because of their length.

Ethan established a mindset for independence from New York and New Hampshire and for the Vermont Constitution. His ideas had mixed with many of the representatives in Bennington, Dorset, Windsor, and other towns during the 1770s. Before Ethan was captured in

1775, his years of leadership as the leader of the Green Mountain Boys, and his verbal persuasion no doubt played a role in the creation of the new republic. His brother Ira, credited with writing or co-writing the Vermont Constitution, was undoubtedly intimately conversant with Ethan's ideas and mindset. Ethan's extensive writing and leadership shaped Vermont's birth.

For example, the first piece on the list, "A Brief Narrative on the Proceedings...," was an organized and reasoned response to the ejectment trials in Albany where Allen had represented New Hampshire grant holders who were being prosecuted civilly by New York patent holders. New York had brought suit against several Grants settlers to evict them or force them to pay fees to New York or their New York patent-holding landlords per New York law. The defendants asked Allen to represent them, and he did so, along with a couple of attorneys who represented some large out-of-state landholders. [12]

In response to Benning Wentworth selling off 130 townships in the Grants, New York had created "paper towns" in the Grants territory. Historian Bob Bass believes New York' had established their eastern boundary 20 miles from the Hudson River, called "the 20-mile line," not the Connecticut River boundary, which New York officials claimed. New York and Massachusetts had agreed to the line many years before the 1770 ejectment trials. The 20-mile line boundary would have ensured the Grants (present-day Vermont) were in New Hampshire territory. Using this thinking, Bass says New York did not have a right to the land east of the line and within the Grants, as they claimed. However, other historians believe New York had a bulletproof case that the Grants belonged to New York. [13]

Legal scholar Gary Shattuck points out in his book with John Duffy and Nick Muller, *The Rebel and the Tory*, that Allen and the defendants had no legal ground to stand on during the ejectment trials. In Shattuck's view, the 20-mile line had only applied to the Massachusetts boundary. According to Shattuck, the New York patents predated the New Hampshire grants, plain and simple. The burden of proof was on the defendants to show the New Hampshire grants were valid, which

Allen failed to do. Since he had no legal argument to defend the validity of the New Hampshire grants, it was an open-and-shut case. Ultimately, the New York judge ruled in favor of New York in the ejectment trials. Allen's strategy of fighting the decision using a different argument wouldn't be the first time or the last time a defendant attempted to win a case without legal grounds. [14]

There is some question about Allen's sentiments after the court decision since Allen and New York attorney James Duane wrote different accounts of their post-trial conversations. A subsequent meeting of Grants holders in Bennington resulted in a robust community commitment to fight New York's implementation of the court's decision on their home turf in the Grants. Since Allen and the other Grants holders had lost their fight in court, Ethan's strategy was to create a propaganda machine with a different rationale to solidify their rightful ownership and vindicate the Grants settlers. [15,16]

Many wealthy nonresidents from other colonies bought New Hampshire grant titles, similar to today's nonresident ownership in some parts of the Green Mountain state. Allen's lengthy narrative pointed out what he called the greedy New York aristocracy attempting to steal land away from hard-working people who had legitimately bought land from New Hampshire Governor Wentworth. Allen wisely identified the grantees as being loyal to the king. He pointed out they were yeomen (working-class farmers) who owned their rightfully purchased land, in contrast to the wealthy absentee landlords of New York, who were often given tens of thousands of acres as perks and gifts. At the time, yeomen were hard-working small-scale farmers who wanted a chance at an 18th-century American dream. [17]

In 1770, virtually all of the residents of the northeast were the king's subjects. Two wealthy governors assumed ownership of the same territory: New York to the west and New Hampshire to the east. Both had claimed ownership and the right to sell grants and land patents in the Grants. This issue was nothing new since Massachusetts had established a town on the Connecticut River (present-day Westminster) and Vernon in the southeast corner of the Grants, which they later relinquished to Vermont.

At the time, no one knew how the New York-Vermont conflict would end, and at the time it would have seemed inconceivable that the Grants would somehow become its separate colony. Scholar Gary Shattuck called this complex dynamic and set of facts a "Gordian knot." Any scenario where Vermont ultimately became a state must have seemed far-fetched and a remarkable achievement to observers.

Having lost the ejectment cases in court, getting no support from New Hampshire, and having limited resources, Allen and the Boys did everything they could to keep the New York sheriffs from doing their jobs in the Grants. Ethan began using his best assets: a talent for blistering rhetoric, intimidating threats, and tapping into moral sentiments.

Ethan created a narrative portraying the New Yorkers as greedy aristocrats trying to intimidate the hard-working Vermonters, which may have been accurate. In his piece called "A Narrative & c.," Ethan described the plaintiff Yorkers "appearing in great Fashion and State... with their Fraternity of Land-monopolizers, [who] made a brilliant appearance. But the Defendants appearing in but ordinary Fashion, having been greatly fatigued by hard Labour,... made a very disproportionable Figure at Court." Allen complained that New York was trying to make examples out of the defendants and frighten the rest so they would comply. [18]

Allen's arguments provided moral support for the grantees and plausible reasons to believe in an alternate reality: they could stubbornly resist the Yorkers and hold onto their property. It was also a powerful public statement that the New York governor and assembly probably did not predict. Members of Congress, governors, other leaders, and the general public read Allen's writing throughout New York and the Grants towns. Even though their legal argument failed, Allen was persuasive in building a solid position and belief in success for the grant holders, forcefully backed up by the Green Mountain Boys using strong-arm tactics. They terrorized Loyalists with humiliation. In one case, a mock trial verdict sentenced former Green Mountain Boy-turned-Loyalist Justus Sherwood to life in the Simsbury, Connecticut, copper mine. Sherwood subsequently escaped and became a British spy for the British Army.

Not long after the British released Allen from confinement in 1778, Ethan acted as state's attorney in the trial of a Loyalist named David Reddington, who the Green Mountain Boys convicted and hanged in Old Bennington, across the road from the Catamount Tavern. This is a controversial chapter in the history of the Green Mountain Boys. But, as other historians point out, the Boys were fighting a guerilla war with the Yorkers, who had kidnapped and imprisoned several men in the Bennington area and informed and committed some vicious raids with Indians on Vermont towns. In some cases, Loyalists such as Reddington, with protection papers from the British, were acting as sleeper cells in Vermont towns, tipping off the raiders as to the locations of livestock, grain, or other valuables in their towns. [19,20]

New York showed its intent to demand justice legally and by force if necessary and was continually frustrated by the Boys' response. New York's "An Act for preventing tumultuous and riotous Assemblies..." was passed in New York on March 9, 1774. Among other things, the new law prohibited more than two people from assembling in one place. Refusing to disperse was punishable by 12 months in prison without bail. According to the act, resisting a sheriff or other official or destroying property were grounds for the death penalty, executed without the benefit of the clergy. Not only that, but this law, which was referred to as 'The Bloody Acts' by the Grants settlers, put rewards on Allen and his ringleaders to apprehend and imprison them. New York gave Allen and his captains 70 days to surrender. [21]

One month later, Allen responded with "Remarks &c. on some late Laws passed in New-York," which clarified his position and was signed by him and his ringleaders and fellow wanted men, Seth Warner, Remember Baker, Robert Cockran [sic], Peleg Sunderland, John Smith, and Silvanus Brown. All of those men knew that they were considered dangerous leaders and a threat to the intentions of the New York government. Allen reiterated that the Grants settlers had fought for a good cause in the eyes of God and that good and honest men were determined to defend their land and personal safety until his majesty's pleasure (concerning the validity of the New Hampshire Grants) was determined. This had a chilling effect on the New York sheriffs and posses sent into Vermont as enforcers.

Allen proposed that the design of the New York law was to obtain possession of the land in the Grants or turn the people who defended them into outlaws and kill them. His rationale was that if the Yorkers came to kill the Green Mountain Boys, then the Boys would react accordingly with equal force to defend their just rights and property. "We are under necessity of resisting, even unto blood, every person who may attempt to take us, opposing Force by Force... until his Majesty shall graciously be pleased to restore us to the Privileges of Englishmen." [22]

How does Allen's writing relate to the unique Vermont we know today? For one, it shows character. When his opponents won the legal argument, Allen adapted with a different strategy using his strengths. Allen's enemies outmatched him with money, education, and experience, and he was "punching up" a weight class. He played David to New York's Goliath. He stood his ground with charismatic and verbose messages, insisting the New Hampshire deeds were valid and the hard-working Vermont yeomen were worthy of their right to prosper. He persevered and persevered and continued actively writing into the 1780s.

This is not to say Ethan Allen founded Vermont or coded Vermont's DNA single-handedly. His leadership was essential for the synergy of the Green Mountain Boys, the council of safety, the governor's council, and the assembly. Some of the Yorkers had lobbied unsuccessfully to get the British redcoats to march into the Grants and put down the Green Mountain Boys. The reluctance of the British Army to march into the Grants and defeat the Green Mountain Boys afforded germination time for the republic. It put the New York-Vermont conflict on the back burner as New York and Vermont territory fought together as Patriots against a common enemy.

By 1775, the Lexington and Concord bloodshed triggered the

revolution, and the war began. Ethan was captured in Montreal and spent the next two-plus years in prison. New York installed Patriot-friendly leadership, and the war pulled attention away from the conflict between New York and the Grants.

A Sea Change

In 1776, as the war exploded, the Grants continued to act like a state. In 1777, it declared its independence as a distinct new identity, wrote a constitution in Windsor, and petitioned the Continental Congress to join the union as New Connecticut. Shortly after that, a new name, Vermont, was agreed upon. Although it would take Vermont 14 more years, until 1791, to iron out their differences with New York and other states in Congress and find the votes needed to join the union, Allen, the Green Mountain Boys, and elected town and republic leaders laid the groundwork for a unique new state.

Vermont's first colonial leaders were originally from Connecticut and Massachusetts. These men included Allen, his brother Ira, Governor Thomas Chittenden, first cousin Remember Baker, fourth cousin Ebenezer Allen, Seth Warner, Stephen and Jonas Fay, Moses Robinson, and a handful of others who formed a nucleus of leadership in the Bennington-Arlington-Sunderland area that many called the "Arlington Junto." The governor, the Committee of Safety, and the governor's council came from this group. Scholar Patricia Thomas made a case that the group was an oligarchy that controlled Vermont and lasted for a generation. Vermont's 1776 declaration of independence from its neighboring colonies cemented the so-called oligarchy. Unfortunately, the Continental Congress didn't support Vermont's constitution, which was based on Pennsylvania's document. New York's was disinclined to approve backwards statehood that might inspire other challenges to the 13 states. Vermont's anti-slavery language and voting rights didn't further their cause with other colonies. [23,24]

The Old Constitution House in Windsor, Vermont, where the Vermont Constitution was
signed in 1777.
Public domain

But Vermont was different right from the beginning, and there
was an "original something" in Ethan that persists in Vermont today.
Vermont is a distinctly novel state. Vermont was the first to have a
popularly elected convention meeting to produce a constitution that
would be submitted to voters for approval. [25]

We continue to value and cling to a work ethic that drove the
yeoman farmers and their families. We still believe in and promote
small farms. We value solid and independent convictions about issues.
Strong grassroots activism that values the people over corporations
thrives. We value and participate in democracy through local, state,
and national engagement. We carry on the tradition of annual meetings where people speak face-to-face and vote on candidates and issues.
Neighbors help neighbors when natural disasters and other problems
hit. Maybe it's a coincidence, or maybe a correlation stems from the
imprint of Allen and the Green Mountain Boys, the hard work of the

early committees of safety, governor's councils, and assemblies, and our beginnings as the culture of our self-made republic is still alive today.

An Agrarian Work Ethic

Ethan and his siblings' parents raised them as yeoman farmers in rural Connecticut. They and other settlers brought the farming identity and work ethic to the Grants. As Ira said in his autobiography, every farmer was a "mechanic," meaning they needed to be a jack-of-all-trades to successfully build and manage a farm, grow crops, raise animals, and fix things on the frontier. Like many people, the Allens aspired to enjoy a higher standard of living than their upbringings afforded. Most of the Allen siblings worked hard, died young, in their 20s or 30s of smallpox or tuberculosis, and none of them fulfilled their dreams of affluence. Vermont's small-scale agrarian work ethic has persisted as a core value, enterprise, and essential sector of the economy. The work ethic has survived waves of change, modernization, new-age farming practices, products, and development pressures. The agriculture and locavore food industries are an essential leg of the Vermont brand.

Strong Independent Convictions

No one would deny that Ethan Allen possessed strong, independent convictions and was always eager to express them. First, he and the Green Mountain Boys battled the New York aristocrats, including the king's governors, their attorneys, sheriffs, and posses. Allen did so with an unwavering commitment to the validity of the New Hampshire land deeds purchased from Governor Benning Wentworth and later his nephew, Governor John Wentworth.

Allen stood on flimsy legal ground to argue against the Yorkers' land claims in 1770. Even though the defendants lost the ejectment trial court battle, which had implications for the entire Grants, Allen argued convincingly and tirelessly on behalf of fellow New Hampshire grant deed holders to delay New York from claiming and controlling the land and the people. Because of the power of his propaganda, persistence, and intimidation, the New York authorities lost their appetite for enforcement. Allen and the Boys stalled New York's enforcement with their strong convictions and persistently lobbied and negotiated with Congress to win their independence and statehood.

Sticking with their convictions, the prospect of statehood became more likely over time. The Yorker conflict faded to a back-burner dispute over contested Loyalist titles. Moses Robinson, Stephen Rowe Bradley, and other Vermont leaders negotiated a $30,000 payment to New York in 1791 that coincided with Vermont's admission to the union. The payment finally settled the New York property dispute.

Pragmatic Grassroots Activism

As the 'Commandant Colonel' of the Green Mountain Boys in the Bennington area, Ethan Allen was Vermont's first colonial grassroots activist leader. Historians such as Bob Bass see the Bennington resistance as the origin of Vermont. The organization branched out to neighboring towns using principles similar to grassroots activism today. Before the Revolution, the southern Grants towns of Bennington, Pownal, Poultney, Tinmouth, Arlington, Dorset, and Rupert, to name a few, established committees of safety, which were provocative shadow governments organized to rebel against the Yorker sheriffs and British on a local level when the hostilities began.

With simple operating principles, Grants towns elected representatives to meetings that planned and actively created their declaration of independence and constitution for the anticipated fourteenth colony. When the Continental Congress didn't accept Vermont as a state, the independent republic of Vermont operated on its own. Grassroots activism fueled a representative government with local committees of safety, a governor, an assembly, and a governor's council. Ethan and Ira's propaganda and tireless face-to-face lobbying in communities drove the marketing and sustained the momentum of the activism throughout the war and beyond.

Today, citizen activism shapes Vermont's policies, laws, and government. Organized activism pits the power of people against corporations and sometimes the government, resulting in a people's statehouse government. Vermont is known for solid participation in activism for causes that span the political spectrum and human lifespan. Activists range from middle and high school students to older Vermonters.

Engagement in Civic and State Affairs and Causes

Ethan Allen was the lynchpin who mobilized others by example, propaganda, his family commitment, and philosophy. He was a relentless fighter for ordinary people- known as yeomen, pursuing what today is called the American dream. The engagement of the Green Mountain Boys in actively resisting New York aristocrats and building the Grants towns was the first organized action against New York and, eventually, what many Vermonters' saw as the tyranny of the king. Allen's relentless energy inspired and mobilized Vermonters to become engaged.

Vermont's constitution engaged more of its population than other states in decision-making and voting rights. While some American colonies limited voting to a subset of male property owners with a certain threshold of land ownership, all Vermont men were allowed to vote. Vermont's early constitution was considered to be progressive at the time. Today, Vermont is known as a state with a high level of voting opportunities, participation, and engagement by all citizens. [26,27]

Annual Town Meetings

Vermont's tradition of holding town meetings to work together to solve town and state, national, and global problems began in the 1770s with the first colonial proprietors' and settlers' meetings. Unlike most states, many Vermont municipalities continue the town meeting tradition of direct and deliberative rule every year. As in the past, town meetings are a forum to meet neighbors face to face, debate issues on principles, and vote on officers, proposals, and referendums. Town meetings are a democracy for and by the people. [28]

Ethan's valuable traits during the Grants and early Vermont period included charisma, a tireless work ethic, strong beliefs and convictions, a confrontational personality, persistence, and a belief in freedom, unity, and democracy. Together with other leaders, their pragmatic activism drove active community engagement in a participatory democracy at the community level. He mobilized and inspired his extended family and the Green Mountain Boys, including his siblings, Heman and Ira, Thomas Chittenden, and many other activists who served in leadership positions. Vermont's constitution infused these ideals and supported the Grants settlers and the new republic that would become the state of Vermont. Those Vermont traditions were early hallmarks of the Allens and the Green Mountain Boys, which have been and still are part of Vermont's ethos after 250 years. Ethan Allen and the Green Mountain Boys programmed Vermont's DNA during the time it became an independent republic through its emergence as our 14th state. That distinct original something is still with us today.

Notes

Introduction
1. Holbrook, Ethan Allen.
2. Bellesiles, Revolutionary Outlaws...
3 Randall, Ethan Allen...
4. Pell, Ethan Allen.
5. Duffy and Muller, Inventing Ethan Allen.
6. Duffy, Muller and Shattuck, The Rebel and the Tory...
7. Whitfield, The Problem of Slavery in Vermont.

Chapter 1
1. Hosley and Ermenc, Household Furnishings and ...
2. Bellesiles, Revolutionary Outlaws...
3. Ibid.
4. Bellesiles, The Autobiography of Levi Allen.
5. Ungeheuer, et al., Roxbury Remembered.
6. Graffagnino, Revolution and Empire on the Northern Frontier...
7. Wilbur and Allen, Founder of Vermont/ Ira Allen Autobiography.
8. Ibid.
9. Ibid.
10. Ibid.
11. Ibid.
12. Ibid.
13. Budde, Arlington, Vermont...
14. Graffagnino, Revolution and Empire on the Northern Frontier...
15. Barr, The Genealogy of Ethan Allen...

Chapter 2
1. Allen, Reason The Only Oracle of Meaning...
2. Thomas, The Hoosac Valley News.
3. Kolenda, Rediscovering Ethan Allen's and Thomas Young's...
4. Bellesiles, Revolutionary Outlaws.

5. Ibid.

6. Maier, Reason and Revolution...

7. Salisbury Justice Records.

8. Ibid.

9. Duffy and Muller, Inventing Ethan Allen.

10. Crown v. William Prendergast, Historical Society of the New York Courts.

11. Wilbur and Allen, Founder of Vermont/ Ira Allen Autobiography...

12. Spargo, Notes on the Ancestors...

12. Ibid.

13. Duffy, Muller, and Shattuck, The Rebel and the Tory...

14. Muller, Vermont's God's of the Hills... p. 125.

15. Duane Journal.

16. Randall, Ethan Allen.

17. Buehner, Green Mountain Women.

18. Joslin, et al., The History of the Town of Poultney.

19. Wilbur and Allen, Founder of Vermont/ Ira Allen Autobiography.

20. Ethan Allen to Levi Allen, Hartford Courant, July 27, 1777.

21. Spargo, Notes on the Ancestors...

22. Beebe, Journal of a Physician...

Chapter 3

1. Randall, Ethan Allen.

2. Buehner, Green Mountain Women.

3. Pell, Ethan Allen.

4. Stevens Papers, Depositions of Jonathan Clap.

5. Ibid.

6. Buehner, Green Mountain Women.

7. Ibid.

8. Spargo, Notes on the Ancestors ....

9. Thomas, The Hoosac Valley News.

10. An Account of the Rise and Progress of the Episcopal Church in Roxbury.

11. Budde, Arlington's History.

12. Canfield, Letter.

13. Hemenway, The Vermont Historical Gazetteer, vol. 1, p. 239.

14. Barr, The Genealogy of Ethan Allen...

15. Buehner, Green Mountain Women.

16. Hitchcock, Ethan Allen, 50 Years in Camp and Field.

17. Ibid.

17. Spargo, Notes on the Ancestors...

18. Barr, The Genealogy of Ethan Allen...

Chapter 4

1. Durfee and Sanford, A Guide to the Henry Stevens, Sr. Collection...
2. Heman Allen to Philip Schuyler.
3. Wilbur and Allen, Founder of Vermont/ Ira Allen Autobiography...
4. Ibid.
5. Ibid.
6. Johnson, The Johnson House.
7. Ibid.
8. Lucinda Catlin Obituary.
9. Spargo, Notes on the Ancestors...
10. Barr, The Genealogy of Ethan Allen...
11. Bellesiles, Life, Liberty, and Land...
12. Heman Allen Will.
13. Barr, The Genealogy of Ethan Allen...

Chapter 5

1. Wilbur and Allen, Founder of Vermont/ Ira Allen Autobiography.
2. Spargo, Notes on the Ancestors...
3. Barr, The Genealogy of Ethan Allen...
4. Ibid.
5. Wilbur, Allen, 2:95.
6. John Allen Finch to Ira Allen, letter.
7. Barr, The Geneaology of Ethan Allen...
8. Beebe, "Journal of a Physician..."
9. Barr, The Genealogy of Ethan Allen...
10. Lucy Allen Beebe, Findagrave.com

Chapter 6

1. Barr, The Genealogy of Ethan Allen...
2. Joslin et al., The History of the Town of Poultney.
3. Ibid.
4. Hemenway, The Vermont Historical Gazetteer, vol. 3, p. 964.
5. 200 Years of History in Vermont, Poultney Historical Society.
6. Jenks, The Women and Children of Poultney.
7. Spargo, Notes on the Ancestors...
8. Ibid.
9. Major Heber Allen, Findagrave.com.
10. Spargo, Notes on the Ancestors...
11. Durfee and Sanford, A Guide to the Henry Stevens, Sr. Collection...
12. Hitchcock, Ethan Allen, 50 Years in Camp and Field.
13. Barr, The Genealogy of Ethan Allen...
14. Major Heber Allen, Findagrave.com.

Chapter 7

1. Nancy Allen to Levi Allen, in Duffy et al., Ethan Allen and His Kin...
2. Buehner, Green Mountain Women
3. Levi Allen to George Washington.
4. Bellesiles, Levi Allen's Autobiography.
5. Ibid.
6. Hitchcock, 50 Years in Camp and Field...
7. Cockerham, B. F., "Levi Allen:...
8. Ibid.
9. Buehner, Green Mountain Women.
10. Allen, (Levi): poetry, original and copies.

Chapter 8

1. Buehner, Green Mountain Women.
2. Spargo, Notes on the Ancestors...
3. Zimri Allen Will.
4. Bellesiles, Life, Liberty, and Land...
5. Zimri Allen Will.

Chapter 9

1. Graffagnino, Revolution and Empire on the Northern Frontier...
2. Wilbur and Allen, Founder of Vermont/ Ira Allen Autobiography.
3. Ibid.
4. Graffagnino, Revolution and Empire on the Northern Frontier.
5. Ira Allen to Ozi Baker, Deed
6. Wilbur and Allen, Founder of Vermont/ Ira Allen Autobiography.
7. Ibid.
8. Himelhoch, The Allens in Early Vermont.
9. Ira Allen to the Vermont Legislature.
10. Graffagnino, Revolution and Empire on the Northern Frontier.
11. Shattuck, email, February 22, 2024.
12. Graffagnino, email, February 22, 2024.
13. Graffagnino, email, February 22, 2024.
14. Graffagnino, Revolution and Empire on the Northern Frontier.
15. Spargo, Notes on the Ancestors...
16. Barr, The Genealogy of Ethan Allen...

Chapter 10

1. Budde, Arlington's History...
2. Thomas, Dave, (Compiler), *The Hoosac Valley News.*
3. George Washington to Ethan Allen.

4. Ethan Allen to George Washington.

5. Budde, Arlington's History...

6. Hayward, A Gazetteer of Vermont...

7. Bellesiles, Life, Liberty, and Land...

8. Buehner, Green Mountain Women.

9. Canadian Archives, B-54, p. 378.

10. Petersen, Otter Creek; The Indian Road.

11. Pemberton, Justus Sherwood, Vermont Loyalist...

12. Bellesiles Life, Liberty, and Land.

13. Ibid.

14. Ibid.

15. Kolenda, Re-Discovering Ethan Allen and Thomas Young's Reason...

16. Lynch and Moira. (Ed.) The Perfectly Acceptable Practice of Literary Theft...

17. Bellisiles, Life, Liberty, and Land...

18. Barlett, A Body Writ...

19. Ibid.

20. Ibid.

21. Ibid.

22. Bellesiles, Life, Liberty, and Land...

23. Bryan, Fanny Allen and Her Children.

Chapter 11

1. Bryan, Fanny Allen and Her Children.

2. Ethan Allen to Crean Brush, Letter.

3. Wiser, Hell's Half-Acre: The Fall of Loyalist Crean Brush.

4. Durfee and Sanford, A Guide to the Henry Stevens, Sr. Collection...

5. Stephen Rowe Bradley to Ethan Allen, Invoice.

6. Bryan, Fanny Allen and Her Children.

7. Sabine, Biographical Sketches of Loyalists...

8. Ethan Allen, Marriage Announcement, *Vermont Gazette.*

9. Udney Hay Papers, VHS.

Chapter 12

1. Bryan, Fanny Allen and her Children.

2. Hemenway, Vermont Historical Gazetteer, History of Burlington.

3. EAHM Property Owners, EAHM Archives, n.d.

4. James Claghorn and the State of Vermont to Ira Allen.

5. Ira Allen to Josiah Averil and Thomas Butterfield, Articles of Agreement.

6. Ozi Baker to Levi Allen.

7. Ethan Allen to Levi Allen, Letter, January 29, 1787, EA&K.

8. Thomas Butterfield to Ira Allen, Letter, April 25, 1785.

9. James Hawley contract to Ira Allen, Allen Family Papers, UVMSC.

10. Reuben, "Chapter 2: Early American Literature."

11. Ethan Allen to St. John deCrevecoeur, Letter, UVMSC.

12. Ethan Allen and Ira Allen, Termination Agreement.

13. Ethan Allen to Levi Allen, June 3, 1787, EA&K.

14. Encouragement for Settling on Onion River, *Vermont Gazette.*

Chapter 13

1. Ethan Allen Hitchcock, 50 Years of Camp and Field.

2. Hemenway, *The Vermont Historical Gazetteer*, vol. 1.

3. Huldah Lawrence Statement.

4. Duffy, et. al., Ethan Allen & Kin.

5. Nancy Allen to Ethan Allen, Letter.

6. Ira Allen to Levi Allen, Letter, July 6, 1787 in Duffy, et. al., Ethan Allen & Kin

7. Henry Collins Statement.

8. Ethan Allen to Royall Tyler, Letter.

9. Peladeau, Royall Tyler and Ethan Allen's Appendix...

10. Ethan Allen to Stephen Rowe Bradley, letter, November 16, 1787.

11. Woolson, To Ethan Allen, Esq., letter.

12. Allen, Ethan, An Essay on The Universal Plentitude.

13. Perkins, Nathan, 1748-1838: A narrative...

14. Levi Allen to Henry Cull.

15. Ethan Allen to Levi Allen, receipt.

16. Ethan Allen to John Wheelock, letter, August 25, 1788, p. 279-280.

17. John Wheelock to Ethan Allen, letter, February 13, 1789, p 291.

Chapter 14

1. Fanny Allen, Inventory of Personal Property.

2. Stevens, Ethan Allen Homestead Museum notes.

3. Ibid.

4. Ibid.

5. Ibid.

6. Ibid.

7. Ibid.

8. Ibid.

9. Wilbur and Allen, Founder of Vermont/ Ira Allen Autobiography.

10. Huldah Lawrence Statement.

11. Hawley Witters Statement.

12. Huldah Lawrence Statement.

13. Barr, The Genealogy of Ethan Allen...

Chapter 15

1. Records and Normals, National Weather Service.

2. Henry Collins Statement.

3. Hawley Witters Statement.

4. Huldah Lawrence Statement.

5. Wilbur and Allen, Founder of Vermont/ Ira Allen Autobiography.

6. Lavados, et. al., Ambient Temperature and Stroke Risk.

7. Huldah Lawrence Statement.

8. Ibid.

Chapter 16

1. Henry Collins Statement.

2. Ibid.

3. Huldah Lawrence Statement.

4. Ethan Allen Funeral, Vermont Gazette.

5. Ibid.

6. Henry Collins Statement.

7. Huldah Lawrence Statement.

8. Ira Hayden Allen to John N. Pomeroy, letter.

9. Ethan Allen's Remains Found, Burlington Free Press.

10. Larkin Goldsmith Mead to George Perkins Marsh and John Norton Pomeroy

11. Vermont Journal, March 9, 1789, p. 37.

12. Silas Hathaway to Ira Allen, letter.

13. Bryan, Fanny and Her Children.

14. Spargo, Notes on the Ancestors...

15. Ibid.

16. Barr, The Genealogy of Ethan Allen...

17. Ethan Alphonso Allen, Findagrave.com.

18. Spargo, Notes on the Ancestors...

19. Bryan, Fanny and Her Children.

20. Ibid.

21. Samuel Hitchcock to Lucy Allen Hitchcock, letter.

22. Bryan, Fanny Allen and Her Children.

Chapter 17

1. Bryan, Fanny and Her Children.

2. Vermont Census, 1990.

3. Bryan, Fanny and Her Children.

4. Smith, Martha Votey, An Early Vermont Botanist.

5. Jabez Penniman to Ira Allen, letter.

6. Ira Allen to Fanny Penniman, letter.

7. Graffagnino, Revolution and Empire on the Northern Frontier.

8. Jabez Penniman to Stephen Rowe Bradley.

9. Ethan Alphonso Allen to Zimry Allen, letter.

10. Allen, Ethan, To The President, letter, April 15, 1808, Burlington Sentinel.

11. Rann, The History of Chittenden County.

12. Barr, The Genealogy of Ethan Allen.

13. Penniman, Jabez, Findagrave.com

Chapter 18

1. Bryan, Fanny Allen and Her Children.

2. Spargo, Notes on the Ancestors...

3. Bryan, Fanny and Her Children.

4. Jacob, Taking the Veil, *The Washingtonian*, Windsor VT, April 15, 1811, pg. 3.

5. Barr, The Genealogy of Ethan Allen...

6. Ibid.

7. Lorraine Hitchcock Peters, Obituary.

8. Barr, The Genealogy of Ethan Allen...

9. Cohen, Ethan Allen Hitchcock, Proceedings...

10. Barr, The Genealogy of Ethan Allen...

11. True, Slavery in Burlington? An Historical Note...

12. Barr, The Genealogy of Ethan Allen...

Chapter 19

1. Walton, Records of the Governor.

2. Henry Collins Statement.

3. Webster's Dictionary 1828.

4. Fanny Allen, Inventory of Personal Property of Ethan Allen.

5. Allen, Ethan, Allen, Ira. Graffagnino, Kevin (Ed.), *Collected Works in 3 Volumes*.

6. Whitfield, The Problem With Slavery in Early Vermont.

7. Ethan Allen to Levi Allen, Letter.

8. Hawley Witters, letter.

9. Goodrich, A Reminiscence.

10. Levi Allen to Jacob A. Lansingh, letter.

11. Bellesiles, Revolutionary Outlaws...

12. Allen, Ethan, Allen, Ira. Graffagnino, Kevin (Ed.), *Collected Works in 3 Volumes*.

13. Whitfield, The Problem With Slavery in Early Vermont, p. 10.

14. Goodrich, Classical Club, University of Vermont.

15. Goodrich, A Reminesince.

16. Oulette, Susan, email.

17. Guyette, Elise, email.

18. Whitfield, The Problem With Slavery in Early Vermont.

19. Guyette, Elise, Black Lives and White Racism in Vermont.

20. Hardesty, email.

21. Cothren, The Ancient Town of Woodbury.

22. Lang, The Plantation Next Door.

23. Connecticut State Archives Archival Record Groups.
24. Cornwall's Connection to "12 Years a Slave."
25. Trumbull, James Russell, History of Northampton...
26. Ibid.
27. Cornwall's Connection to "12 Years a Slave."
28. Holcomb, "How 18th-Century Quakers..."
29. Washington Post, "More than 1,800 congressmen once enslaved..."
30. Fay, Vermont's Ebenezer Allen...
31. Stephen Rowe Bradley: A Featured Biography.
32. Crèvecur, Saint John de Crèvecur, sa vie et ses ouvrages...
33. True, Marshall. "Slavery in Burlington? An Historical Note."
34. Potash, Jeffery. Project Honoring Enslaved Vermonters...
35. Hardesty, email.
36. Whitfield, North to Bondage.
37. Guyette, email.

Chapter 20

1. Petersen, *Otter Creek: The Indian Road*.
2. Calloway, Colin G., "The Conquest of Vermont..."
3. Fay, Vermont's Ebenezer Allen...
4. Allen, Ethan. Letter of Ethan Allen to the Indians of Canada.
5. Ibid.
6. Bellesiles, Revolutionary Outlaws.
7. Ethan Allen to Philip Schuler, letter.
8. Ibid.
9. Graffagnino, Kevin, draft comment, March 9, 2024.
10. Wilbur and Allen, Founder of Vermont/ Ira Allen Autobiography.
11. Haviland and Power, Original Vermonters.
12. Ibid.

Chapter 21

1. Freedom & Unity: A Graphic Guide to Civics and Democracy in Vermont.
2. Bellesiles, Revolutionary Outlaws, p.162-3.
3. Bass, email.
4. Shattuck, email.
5. Shattuck, Law "at the Muzzle of the Gun," ..
6. Shattuck, email.
7. Bellesiles, email.
8. Abigail Allen Wadhams, Deposition.
9. Graffagnino, email.
10. Duffy, Muller and Shattuck, The Rebel and the Tory...
11. Ethan Allen to The Public, Duffy et al., Ethan Allen & His Kin, p. 164

12. Allen, Ethan, Allen, Ira. Graffagnino, Kevin (Ed.), *Collected Works in 3 Volumes.*

13. Bass, email.

14. Duffy, Muller and Shattuck, The Rebel and the Tory...

15. Ibid.

16. Bass, email.

17. Allen, Ethan, Allen, Ira. Graffagnino, Kevin (Ed.), *Collected Works in 3 Volumes,*

18. Ibid., p4.

19. Bellesiles, Revolutionary Outlaws...

20. Spargo, The Story of David Redding Who was Hanged.

21. Allen, Ethan, Allen, Ira. Graffagnino, Kevin (Ed.), *Collected Works in 3 Volumes*

22. Ibid.

23. Thomas, Patricia, "A Study in Familial Ties in Early Vermont Government."

24. Duffy, Muller, and Shattuck, The Rebel and the Tory...

25. Bellesiles, Revolutionary Outlaws..., p. 258.

26. Whitfield, The Problem of Slavery in Early Vermont.

27. Bellesiles, Revolutionary Outlaws...

28. Bryan, Frank M., Real Democracy.

Bibliography

200 Years of History in Vermont, Poultney Historical Society, 2022.

Abigail Wadhams, deposition, *Moses Catlin & Lucinda Catlin vs Ira Allen*, US Circuit Court, District of Vermont, Oct. 1798, RG 21, Box 2, National Archives and Records Administration, Boston, MA.

Allen, Ethan, Allen, Ira. Graffagnino, Kevin (Ed.), *Collected Works in 3 Volumes*, Chaldize Productions, 1992.

Allen, Ethan, *A Narrative of Colonel Ethan Allen's Captivity*. Philadelphia; Robert Bell, 1779.

Allen, Ethan, *An Essay on The Universal Plentitude of Being and on the Nature of Immortality of the Human Soul and its Agency,* digital images of original, [1784] Colonial Library of North America at Harvard University.

Allen, Ethan, "An Essay on The Universal Plentitude of Being and on the Nature of Immortality of the Human Soul and its Agency," *The Historical Magazine* And Notes And Queries Concerning the Antiquities, History And Biography of America, Morrisania, N.Y. [etc.]: Henry B. Dawson [etc.], #209 (p. 193).

Allen, Ethan. Letter of Ethan Allen to the Indians of Canada, Three Roots Press Poster Series, No. 5, B4, F27, *Allen Family Papers, UVMSC*, May 14, 1775.

Allen, Ethan, *Reason the Only Oracle of Man*, Anthony Haswell, Bennington, 1784.

Allen, Ethan, To The President, letter, April 15, 1808, Burlington Sentinel.

Allen, Levi: poetry, original and copies, *Allen Family Papers, UVMSC*, 29: 59, n.d.

Allen, Levi, "Twenty Dollars Reward," *Hartford Courant,* November 3, 1778.

"An Account of the Rise and Progress of the Episcopal Church in Roxbury," *Churchman's Monthly Magazine*, vol. 2, no. 10 (New Haven, CT; Comstock, Griswold & Co., 1805), 224.

Austin, Aleine (1981). Matthew Lyon: "New Man" of the Democratic Revolution. 1749-1822, Pennsylvania State University Press, 1981.

Barr, John, *The Genealogy of Ethan Allen and His Brothers and Sisters*, Ethan Allen Homestead Trust, 1983.

Bartlett, H. O., 1889, "A Body Writ for Arrest of Gen. Ethan Allen," *Burlington Daily Free Press*, August 21, 1889, Newspapers.com.

Bass, Bob, email, June 2023.

Beebe, Dr. Lewis, "Journal of a Physician on the Expedition against Canada, 1776," *The Pennsylvania Magazine of History and Biography, Volume LIX*, Oct 1935, Number 4.

Bellesiles, Michael A. "Life, Liberty, and Land: Ethan Allen and the Frontier Experience in Revolutionary New England" Thesis (Ph. D., History)--University of California, Irvine, 1986.

Bellesiles, Michael A., email, September 24, 2023.

Bellesiles, Michael A. *Revolutionary Outlaws: Ethan Allen and the Struggle for Independence on the Early American Frontier*, University of Virginia Press, 1993.

Bellesiles, Michael A. (Ed.), The Autobiography of Levi Allen, Vermont Historical Society, Spring 1992, vol. 60 no. 2.

Bennington, Vermont. Old First Congregational Church records, 1752-1937, Church records, 1762-1820, Old First Congregational Church of Bennington, Vt, p. 38

Brown, Charles Walter. *Ethan Allen*. Chicago: M. A. Donohue & Co., 1902.

Bryan, David, *Fanny and Her Children*, Manuscript, Ethan Allen Homestead Museum, 1985.

Bryan, Frank M., *Real Democracy*, University of Chicago Press. pp. 213–231, 2003.

Budde, William. *Arlington, Vermont: Its First 250 Years,* Arlington Townscape Association, 2014.

Buehner, Terry L, "Green Mountain Women," Master's Thesis, University of Vermont, 1992.

Canadian Archives, B-54, p. 378.

Calloway, Colin G., "The Conquest of Vermont: Vermont's Indian Troubles in Context, " VHS, Summer 1984, vo. 52 no. 3.

Canfield, H. H., Letter, *Vermont Historical Society Library,* AS 116 1943.

Carter, Joseph C., "In the Name of God, Amen!" *Allen Family Papers, UVMSC,* 28-1.

Cawley, David, Email interview, October 13, 2023.

Cockerham, B. F., "Levi Allen (1746-1801): Opportunism and the Problem of Allegiance," M.A. Thesis, University of Vermont, 1965.

Cohen, L.B., Ethan Allen Hitchcock, Proceedings of the American Antiquarian Society, 1951.

Connecticut State Archives Archival Record Groups (RG) #003, Connecticut State Library.

Cornwall's Connection to "12 Years a Slave," The Register Citizen, January 25, 2014.

Cothren, William, *The Ancient Town of Woodbury,* Woodbury, Connecticut,1872, p. 319.

Crèvecur, Robert St. John de, *Saint John de Crèvecur, sa vie et ses ouvrages (1735-1813) avec les portraits de Crèvecur et de la comtesse d'Houdetot, gravés d'après des miniatures du temps1833,* Paris Library, Univeriversity of Pittsburgh, 1833.

"Crown v. William Prendergast, 1766." *Historical Society of the New York Courts,* State of New York, 6 Aug. 2019, history.nycourts.gov.

Drew, Bernard, "Zimri, the other Allen brother," *Berkshire Eagle,* June 30, 2018.

Duane Journal, *Duane Family Papers, NYHS*, Series 4: Bound volumes, 1754-1843, pp. 203-4.

Duffy, John, Muller, H. Nicholas, *Inventing Ethan Allen*, University Press of New England, 2014.

Duffy, John, Muller, H. Nicholas, Shattuck, Gary G., *The Rebel And The Tory: Ethan Allen, Philip Skene, and the Dawn of Vermont*, Vermont Historical Society, 2020.

Duffy, John, Orth, Ralph, Graffagnino, Kevin, and Michael A Bellesiles (Eds.) *Ethan Allen and His Kin: Correspondence 1772-1819*. Hanover and London: University Press of New England, 1998.

Durfee, Eleazer, Sanford, Gregory. *A Guide to the Henry Stevens, Sr. Collection at the Vermont State Archives*, NEH, n.d.

EAHM Property Owners, EAHM Archives, n.d.

Encouragement for Settling on Onion River, *Vermont Gazette*, May 9, 1787.

Ethan Allen and Ira Allen, Termination Agreement, May 1, 1787, *EAHM Collection*, Transcribed by Phillip Bowler, UVM, 12/19/1990.

Ethan Allen Funeral, *Vermont Gazette*, March 16, 1789.

Ethan Allen to Crean Brush, Letter, May 8, 1774, *Allen Family Papers, UVMSC*, 3-67.

Ethan Allen to The Public, in Duffy, et. al., *Ethan Allen & His KIn*, vol. 1, p. 164.

Ethan Allen, marriage announcement, *Vermont Gazette*, February 21, 1784.

Ethan Allen's Remains Found, *Burlington Free Press*, June 18, 1858.

Ethan Allen to George Washington, letter, May 28, 1778, *founders.archives.gov*.

Ethan Allen to Hector St. John deCrevecoeur, letter, April 4, 1787, *Allen Family Papers, UVMSC*, 4-58.

Ethan Allen to Levi Allen, letter, June 3, 1787, in Duffy, et al., *Ethan Allen and His Kin*, 1:177.

Ethan Allen to Levi Allen, letter, July 27, 1777, *Hartford Courant*.

Ethan Allen to Levi Allen, letter, Nov. 6, 1788, in Duffy, et al., *Ethan Allen and His Kin.*.

Ethan Allen to Levi Allen, receipt, June 15, 1787, *Allen Family Papers, UVMSC.*

Ethan Allen to Philip Schuyler, letter, September 8, 1775, *Allen Family Papers, UVMSC.*

Ethan Allen to Royall Tyler, letter, August 28, 1787, *Allen Family Papers, UVMSC.*

Ethan Allen to Stephen Rowe Bradley, letter, November 16, 1787, in Duffy et al., Ethan Allen and His Kin, p. 289.

Ethan Alphonso Allen, Findagrave.

Ethan Alphonso Allen, letter, *Burlington Sentinel and Democrat*, April 15, 1808.

Ethan Alphonso Allen to Zimry Allen, letter, March 1, 1808, *VHS Library.*

Fanny Allen, Inventory of Personal Property of Ethan Allen, Westminster, Vermont, 1802, Udney Hay Papers, MS 152, *Vermont Historical Society Library.*

Fay, Jr., Glenn, *Hidden History of Burlington, Vermont,* The History Press, 2022.

Fay, Jr., Glenn. *Vermont's Ebenezer Allen: Patriot, Commando, Emancipator,* The History Press, 2021.

Freedom & Unity: A Graphic Guide to Civics and Democracy in Vermont, Vermont Humanities Council, 2022.

French, Allen. *The Taking of Ticonderoga in 1775: The British Story,* rpt of edition published by Harvard University Press, 1928 (Cranbury, N.J.: The Scholar's Bookshelf, 2005), 30–33.

George Washington to Henry Laurens, letter, May 12, 1778, *founders.archives.gov.*

Gerzina, Gretchen Holbrook, *Mr. and Mrs. Prince: How an Extraordinary Eighteenth-Century Family Moved Out of Slavery and into Legend*, Harper Collins, 2009.

"Goodrich Classical Club," University of Vermont, About John Ellsworth Goodrich, 2023, *UVM.edu.*

Goodrich, J.E., "A Reminiscence," essay, n.d. UVM Silver Special Collections, Allen Family Papers, 28-16.

Goodrich, Ellen M. Moody, Findagrave.com.

Graffagnino, J. Kevin, draft comment, March 9, 2024.

Graffagnino, J. Kevin, "Revolution and empire on the northern frontier : Ira Allen of Vermont, 1751-1814." (1993). *Doctoral Dissertations 1896 - February 2014.* 1193. https://doi.org/10.7275/72ha-7476.

Graffagnino, J. Kevin, email, February 22, 2024.

Graffagnino, J. Kevin, email, January 26, 2024.

Graffagnino, J. Kevin, "Revolution and empire on the northern frontier: Ira Allen of Vermont, 1751-1814." (1993). *Doctoral Dissertations 1896 - February 2014.* 1193.

Greene, Lorenzo Johnston, *The Negro in Colonial New England, 1620-1776.* N.Y.: Columbia University Press, 1942, p.74-75.

Guyette, Elise, *Black Lives and White Racism in Vermont: 1760-1870*, Master's Thesis, University of Vermont, October 1992.

Guyette, Elise, email, August 20, 2023.

Hall, Hiland, *The History of Vermont, From Its Discovery to Its Admission into the Union in 1791*, Joel Munsell, 1868.

Hardesty, Jared, email, July 9, 2021 and August 21, 2023.

Haviland, William A., Power, Marjory W., *The Original Vermonters: Native Inhabitants, Past and Present*, Lebanon, NH, UPNE, 1981.

Hawley Witters, Statement, *Burlington Free Press*, June 19, 1858.

Hayward, John, "History of the Town of Sunderland, VT," *Gazetteer of Vermont*, Hayward, Heritage Books, 1990.

Hayward, John, *A Gazetteer of Vermont...*, Tappen, Whittemore and Mason, 1849.

Heman Allen to Philip Schuyler, letter, *Allen Family Papers, UVMSC*, 4-42.

Heman Allen, Will, Probate District Court, Sharon, Litchfield County, CT.

Hemenway, Abby M., ed., *The Vermont Historical Gazetteer*, 5 vols. (vol. 1: Burlington: Miss A.M. Hemenway, 1867; vol. 2, Burlington: Miss A.M. Hemenway, 1871; vol. 3; Claremont, NH; The Claremont Manufacturing Company, 1877; vol. 4; Montpelier: Vermont Watchman and State Journal Press, 1882; vol. 5: Brandon: Mrs. Carrie E.H. Page, 1891. 1:239)

Henry Collins, statement, June 19, 1858, *Burlington Free Press*.

Himmelhoch, Myra, *The Allens in Early Vermont*, Unpublished manuscript, EAHM, 1967.

Historical collections relating to the town of Salisbury, Litchfield County, Connecticut, The Salisbury Association, Salisbury, CT, 1913.

"Historical Society of the New York Courts, Crown v. William Prendergast," White Plains, NY, nd, *nycourts.gov*.

Hitchcock, Ethan Allen, Croffut, W.A. (Ed.), *Fifty Years in Camp and Field*, Putnam's Sons, New York, 1909, LOC.gov.

Holbrook, Stewart H. *Ethan Allen*. New York: The MacMillian Company, 1940.

Holcomb , Julie. "How 18th-Century Quakers Led a Boycott of Sugar to Protest against Slavery." *The Conversation*, The Conversation, 13 Sept. 2022.

Hosley, Jr., William N., Ermenc, Christine, *Household furnishings and Domestic Economy on the Vermont Frontier: A Plan for Interpreting the Ethan Allen Homestead*, Enfield, CT, Ethan Allen Homestead Museum, 1985.

Huldah Lawrence Statement, *Burlington Free Press*, June 19, 1858.

Ira Allen to Fanny Penniman, letter, June 12, 1802, in Duffy, et al., *Ethan Allen and His Kin*, 1:177.

Ira Allen to Josiah Averil and Thomas Butterfield, Articles of Agreement, *Allen Family Papers, UVMSC*, May 2, 1786.

Ira Allen to Levi Allen, letter, July 6, 1787, in Duffy, et al., Ethan Allen & Kin.

Ira Allen to Ozi Baker, deed, December 10, 1783, *Colchester, VT Land Records.*

Ira Allen to the Vermont Legislature, letter, September 16, 1789, *Allen Family Papers, UVMSC,* 11-111.)

Ira Hayden Allen to John N. Pomeroy, letter, June 14, 1858, UVMSC, *John Norton Pomeroy Papers, UVMSC,* 2, 2-7D.

Jabez Penniman to Ira Allen, letter, February 16, 1802, in Duffy, et al., *Ethan Allen and His Kin,* 1:177.

Jabez Penniman to Stephen Rowe Bradley, letter, March 26, 1804, *Stephen Rowe Bradley Papers, UVMSC.*

Jacob, Laura, "Taking the Veil, Taking the Veil, Fanny Allen's veiling ceremony," *The Washingtonian,* Windsor VT, April 15, 1811, pg. 3

James Claghorn and the State of Vermont to Ira Allen, deed, Vermont Historical Society Library, 1778.

Jellison, Charles A. *Ethan Allen: Frontier Rebel.* Syracuse: Syracuse University Press, 1969, 314-315.

Jenks, Margaret, *The Women and Children of Poultney, Rutland County, Vermont Fleeing Burgoyne's Forces 6 July 1777,* Poultney Historical Society, n.d

John Allen Finch to Ira Allen, letter, June 22, 1791, *Allen Family Papers, UVMSC.*

Johnson House, The University of Vermont, *UVM.edu.*

John Wheelock to Ethan Allen, letter, February 13, 1789, 11-57, *Allen Family Papers, UVMSC.*

Joslin, Joseph, Frisbie, Barnes, Ruggles, Frederick, *A History of the Town of Poultney, Vermont: From Its Settlement to the Year 1875, with Family and Biographical Sketches and Incidents,* Poultney Historical Society, 1875.

Kolenda, Benjamin, "Re-Discovering Ethan Allen and Thomas Young's Reason the Only Oracle of Man: The Rise of Deism in Pre-Revolutionary America." master's thesis, Georgia State University, 2013.

Lang, Joel, "The Plantation Next Door," *Hartford Courant*, September 29, 2002.

Larkin Goldsmith Mead to George Perkins Marsh and John Norton Pomeroy, letter, June 10, 1858, *UVMSC*, cdi.uvm.edu.

Lavados, P, Olavaria, V, Hoffmeister, L, Ambient Temperature and Stroke Risk, AHA Journals, 2017. https://doi.org/10.1161/STROKEAHA.117.017838 Stroke. 2018;49:255–261.

Levi Allen to George Washington, letter, 27 January 1776," *Founders Online,* National Archives, https://founders.archives.gov/documents/Washington/03-03-02-0141. [Original source: *The Papers of George Washington*, Revolutionary War Series, vol. 3, *1 January 1776 – 31 March 1776*, ed. Philander D. Chase. Charlottesville: University Press of Virginia, 1988, pp. 195–197.]

Levi Allen to Henry Cull, letter, *UVMSC*, January 14, 1788.

Levi Allen to Jacob A. Lansingh, letter, Dec. 3, 1784, in Duffy, et al., *Ethan Allen & His Kin*, 1:164.

Levi Allen, advertisement, November 3, 1778, Twenty Dollars Reward, *Hartford Courant.*

Litchfield Cty records, Historical Collections Relating to the Town of Salisbury, Litchfield County, Connecticut, www.wikitree.com.

Lorraine Hitchcock Peters, obituary, May 5, 1815.

Lucinda Allen Catlin, obituary, *Burlington Free Press*, February 2, 1784.

Lynch, Jack., Allen, Moira. (Ed.) "The Perfectly Acceptable Practice of Literary Theft: Plagiarism, Copyright, and the Eighteenth Century," Writing-World.com.

Lynch, James V., "The Limits of Revolutionary Radicalism: Tom Paine and Slavery," The Pennsylvania Magazine of History and Biography, Vol. CXXIII, No. 3, July 1999, journals.psu.edu.

Maier, Pauline. "Reason and Revolution: The Radicalism of Dr. Thomas Young." *American Quarterly* 28, no. 2 (1976): 229–49. https://doi.org/10.2307/2712351.

Main, Jackson Turner, *Society & Economy in Colonial Connecticut*, Princeton University Press, 1983, p.177.

Muller, H. Nicholas, "Vermont's God's of the Hills: Buying Tradition From a Sole Source... ," *Vermont History* Vol. 75, No. 2 (Summer/Fall 2007): 125–133., 2007.

Nancy Allen to Ethan Allen, letter, June 29, 1787, *Allen Family Papers, UVMSC.*

Nancy Allen to Ethan Allen, letter, October 20, 1798, *Allen Family Papers, UVMSC.*

Nancy Allen, Transcribed, copy of a letter by Lawrence Sterne, September 5, 1790, *Allen Family Papers, UVMSC.*

Onion River Map, "Copy of W. Blanchards map of Onion & Lemoil Rivers, Vermont," 4 maps and surveys of traverses along the "Onion", now the Winooski River from Colchester township, 1772" [sic] New York State Library, Albany, NY, Manuscripts and Special Collections, Cockburn Family Land Papers, SC7004, Box 10 of 11.

Oulette, Susan, email, September 22, 2021.

Ozi Baker to Ira Allen, letter, Wilbur collection, Microfilm, UVM.

Pell, John, *Ethan Allen*, Houghton Mifflin, 1929.

Pemberton, Ian Cleghorn, "Justus Sherwood, Vermont Loyalist, 1747-1798" (1973). *Digitized Thesis.* 646.

Peladeau, Marius, "Royall Tyler and Ethan Allen's Appendix to Reason the Only Oracle of Man," Vermont Historical Society, Summer, 1968.

Penniman, George W., Penniman, George D. (Ed.), *The Penniman Family 1631-1900*, Gateway Press, Baltimore, 1981.

Perkins, Nathan, 1748-1838: A narrative of a tour through the state of Vermont from April 27 to June 12, 1789 The Elm Tree Press, 1920.

Petersen, James E., *Otter Creek: The Indian Road*, Dunmore House, Salisbury, Vermont, 1990.

Potash, Jeffery. Project Honoring Enslaved Vermonters Asks State To Confront 'A Dark Side Of Our History,' Hirshfield, Peter, Vermont Public, *Vermont Edition*, August 27, 2020, www.vermontpublic.org.

Proceedings of the Vermont Historical Society For The Years 1913-1914, Vermont Historical Society, Allen family letters- VHS p 188 Ethan jr talks of Ira, 1915.

Randall, Willard Sterne, *Ethan Allen: His Life and Times*, New York, W.W. Norton, 2011.

Rann, William, *The History of Chittenden County*, D. Mason, Syracuse, 1886.

Reuben, Paul P. "Chapter 2: Early American Literature: 1700–1800 – St. Jean De Crevecoeur", *PAL: Perspectives in American Literature – A Research and Reference Guide* https://web.archive.org

Roberts, Lemuel, *Memoirs of Captain Lemuel Roberts*, Anthony Haswell, Bennington, 1809.

"Records and Normals," National Weather Service, weather.gov, n.d.

Sabine, Lorenzo (1864). *Biographical Sketches of Loyalists of the American Revolution: With an Historical Essay* (Public domain ed.). Little, Brown. p. 270.

Samuel Hitchcock to Lucy Allen Hitchcock, Letter, August 28, 1791, Duffy, et al., *Ethan Allen & His Kin*.

Salisbury Justice Records, Salisbury, CT, I: II, 27 October 1765.

Shattuck, Gary, email, August 24, 2023, January 2024.

Shattuck, Gary, email, February 22, 2024.

Shattuck, Gary, "Law 'at the Muzzle of the Gun," Archaeology of Fugitive Terrain. New Hampshire Grants, 1749-1791." *Vermont History Vol. 87*, No. 1, Spring/Summer 2019.

Shattuck, Gary, personal interview by phone, June 1, 2023.

Silas Hathaway to Ira Allen, letter, Vermont Centinel, April 4, 1802.

Smith, Martha Votey, "An Early Vermont Botanist," *The Vermonter*, April 1913.

Spargo, John. *Notes on the Ancestors and Immediate Descendants of Ethan and Ira Allen, Bennington, Allen Family Papers, UVMSC*, 1948.

Spargo, John, *The Story of David Redding Who was Hanged*, "David Redding, Queen's Ranger Who Was Hanged in Bennington, Vermont June 11, 1778," 1945.

Stephen Rowe Bradley: *A Featured Biography*, United States Senate,.senate.gov/senators/

Stephen Rowe Bradley to Ethan Allen, letter, October 25, 1783, *AFP, UVMSC*.

Stevens Papers, Vermont State Archives and Records Administration, "Depositions of Jonathan Clap," June 1767, March 1768.
Stevens, Scott, Ethan Allen Homestead Museum notes, n.d.

Thomas Butterfield to Ira Allen, letter, April 25, 1785, *Allen Family Papers, UVMSC*.

Thomas, Dave, (Compiler), *The Hoosac Valley News*, Heritage Quest Books, Vol. II, P. 70).

Thomas, Patricia Lavery, "A Study in Familial Ties in Early Vermont Government" Master's Thesis, University of Vermont, February 1972.

True, Marshall. "Slavery in Burlington? An Historical Note," Vermont Historical Society, Vol. 50 No. 4, Fall 1982.

Trumbull, James Russell, *History of Northampton, Massachusetts...*, UMass Amherst Libraries, Northampton Press, 1898.

Ungeheuer, Frederick, Hurlburt, Lewis, Hurlburt, Ethel, *Roxbury Remembered*, Connecticut Heritage Press, 1989.

Udney Hay Papers, Vermont Historical Society, MS 152, 1802.

"Vermont Chronology, 1764-1992," University of Wisconsin, CSAC.history.wisc.edu, n.d.

Land for Sale, *Vermont Gazette*, May 9, 1787, newspapers.com.

Vermont Journal, March 9, 1789, p. 37.

Vermont Census, U.S. Census, 1790, census.gov..

Vermont Frontier: A Plan for Interpreting the Ethan Allen Homestead, Enfield, CT, Ethan Allen Homestead Museum, 1985.

Walton, E. P., (Ed.) *Records of the Governor and Council of the State of Vermont: General conventions in the New Hampshire grants . . . July, 1775 to December, 1777. The first constitution of the State of Vermont. Council of Safety . . . July 8, 1777, to March 12, 1778. Record of the Governor and Council, 1778-1779*, Steam Press of J & J M Poland, Montpelier, VT, 1873.

"More than 1,800 congressmen once enslaved Black people. This is who they were, and how they shaped the nation," *Washington Post*, n.d., washingtonpost.com.

Webster's Dictionary 1828, "servant," Masonsoft Technology, 2022, webstersdictionary1828.com.

Whitfield, Harvey Amani, *North to Bondage: Slavery in the Maritimes*, UBC Press, 2016.

Whitfield, Harvey Amani, *The Problem of Slavery in Early Vermont, 1777-1810*, Vermont Historical Society, 2019.

Wilbur, James, Allen, Ira, *Ira Allen: Founder of Vermont, Autobiography*, 2 vols. Houghton Mifflin, Riverside Press, Boston & New York, 1928.

Wiser, Eric. "Hell's Half-Acre: The Fall of Loyalist Crean Brush," *Journal of the American Revolution, All Things Liberty*, January 19, 2022, allthingsliberty.com.

Woolson, To Ethan Allen, Esq., letter, May 5, 1787, *Vermont Gazette*.

Zimry Allen Will, *Probate District Court*, Sharon, Litchfield County, CT.

Abbreviations

AFP- Allen Family Papers
EAHM- Ethan Allen Homestead Museum
NARA- National Archives Records Administration
NYS- New York State
ORLC- Onion River Land Company
UVM- University of Vermont
UVMSC- UVM Special Collections
VHS- Vermont Historical Society
VSARA- Vermont State Records Administration

Glenn Fay is a descendant of Daniel Champion, a Green Mountain Boy, and Jon Powers II, a New Hampshire militiaman, and a native Vermonter. He has researched and written about characters in the American Revolution in Vermont, with two prior books, *Vermont's Ebenezer Allen* and *Hidden History of Burlington, Vermont*, published by The History Press. Glenn serves on the Board of Directors at the Ethan Allen Homestead Museum.

Milton Keynes UK
Ingram Content Group UK Ltd.
UKHW030321090824
446663UK00003B/181